Seed Deals

Seed Deals

How to Grow from Startup
to Venture Capital

DAVID J. WILLBRAND

CAROLINA ACADEMIC PRESS
Durham, North Carolina

Library of Congress Cataloging-in-Publication Data

Names: Willbrand, David J., author.
Title: Seed deals : how to grow from startup to venture capital
/ by David J. Willbrand.
Description: Durham, NC : Carolina Academic Press, 2021.
Identifiers: LCCN 2020056167 (print) | LCCN 2020056168 (ebook)
| ISBN 9781531021283 (paperback) | ISBN 9781531021290 (ebook)
Subjects: LCSH: New business enterprises—Finance. |
Venture capital.
Classification: LCC HG4027.6 .W55 2021 (print) |
LCC HG4027.6 (ebook) | DDC 658.15/224—dc23
LC record available at https://lccn.loc.gov/2020056167
LC ebook record available at https://lccn.loc.gov/2020056168

Carolina Academic Press
700 Kent Street
Durham, North Carolina 27701
Telephone (919) 489-7486
Fax (919) 493-5668
www.cap-press.com

Printed in the United States of America
2024 Printing

To my wife April, and to our children Ella, Ethan, Max and Zoë

Contents

Acknowledgments

Many people contributed to the ideas, substance and structure of this book. It would be futile to try to name them all—but I appreciate you all so much!

As to those who specifically read and shared comments and feedback on various drafts, my heartfelt thanks (and any remaining mistakes remain my own, of course!):

Esther Barron
Erin Borcherding
Jeremy D'Abreau
Shelby Ewing
Michael Fenn
Rachael Feuerborn
Tayler Gill
Christina Heilig
Logan LaHive
Craig Looper
Suzanne McNabb
Michelle Murcia
Margot Seidel
Blake Smith
Shane Starkey
Justin Thompson
Jonathon Vinocur
Paige L. Wilson
Donald Wright
Daniela M. Yoder

I should also mention Tim Holcomb. This book evolved from a presentation I have been sharing with founders, entrepreneurs, investors, students and many others over the years. It's become known as my "ChalkTalk," a name Tim gave it. Without that name, and without the opportunity to refine and perfect that presentation over the years in front of so many of his classes, this book would never have been.

Seed Deals

Introduction

If you are holding this book in your hands, you are one of three things:

* A founder or an entrepreneur (or thinking about it)
* A law student (or thinking about it)
* A startup lawyer (or thinking about it)

Congratulations! You've taken an important step.

Believe it or not, you three have a lot in common. You love startups, and you understand that "the law" plays a role. You come here seeking knowledge. You'll get it!

In the context of a startup, the relationship between founder and lawyer is sacred. It's a partnership—and not just a professional one. It's deeply personal.

And like all partnerships, for it to work well, both parties need to be rooted in the same dirt. This stuff isn't for tourists. It's for those who will roll up their sleeves, grab a shovel, and start digging.

My job? To give you everything you need to grow this garden together.

I will educate you about the dirt. And the sun. And the rain. And the wind.

And I'll provide you with the seeds . . .

* * *

I love to read. I love to teach. I love to practice law and honing those skills.

But do you know what I don't like?

Reading, teaching, or trying to learn from books on finance, on venture capital, on entrepreneurship. Routinely terrible. Their tragedy is exceeded only by books on the law. Snoozefest . . .

My goal here? To cover all these topics in a way that's just a little less terrible or boring (I have found I do best when I set expectations low . . .).

* * *

Entrepreneurs start companies for lots of reasons.

For some, there is a problem they just really want to solve—or people with whom they just really want to work. For others, there is the matter of legacy—they want to create something, and leave something behind. And the list goes on.

And those are all great reasons to start a company!

A terrible reason? To get rich quick. As any entrepreneur will tell you, there are easier ways to make a buck.

That being said—it's entirely reasonable, and appropriate, to start a company for the right reasons but still aspire to cash a check.

That's what this book is about. Teeing-up that financial success.

* * *

This is not a book with tips on product development, marketing, sales, or talent. It's a book on ownership, finance, and raising money. And on how to make sure the founder preserves a healthy piece of the pie.

This stuff shouldn't be that hard. In a perfect world, it wouldn't be. But this world isn't perfect.

Too many JDs, too many MBAs, and yes, just enough scoundrels and sneaky finance types have made this stuff dense and impenetrable. So much jargon. So much weird terminology. All with the intention, at least it seems, of confusing and tricking you.

I am going to fix that here. You may not finish this book an expert, but you'll know enough to do things the right way, to know what to look for (and what to look *out* for)—and how to build a proper startup ownership structure.

* * *

This book is primarily addressed to those in the orbit of tech or life science companies, businesses which are first and foremost focused on product development, intellectual property, and market share more than profits or even revenue. These companies frequently lose money throughout the entirety of their existence. Their reward is at the end of the rainbow—the sale of the company.

For those of you interested or involved in more traditional "Main Street" businesses, where it's less about selling the company and more about day-to-day profits, the high-level concepts described here will certainly carry through. But to be transparent, those businesses don't raise money in the same kind of way, or at the same cadence, and so a lot of the particularities I describe won't be directly applicable.

* * *

What you'll find here is accurate, and it's punchy. My belief is that you should be able to get through this book on a flight from LaGuardia to LAX with time to spare. And then throw the thing into your bag feeling like you learned something, rather than simply endured some boring rite of passage.

This book is meant to be read cover-to-cover. It's not a reference manual per se. It tells a story, and the concepts build. That said, look, you do you! What follows is a taxonomy of this book, and if you want to bounce around, you certainly may.

In Chapter 1, we cover the ***balance sheet*** and how it ties to exit transactions—the place the money is made!

In Chapters 2 and 3, we discuss ***capitalization (or cap) tables***, which articulate the company's ownership structure and provide a map when it comes time to split up the winnings from that exit transaction.

After a quick sidebar on the ***Delaware "C" corporation***, Chapters 4–10 cover ***common shares*** and ***preferred shares***, teasing out the basics of each.

After another sidebar, this one on *Venture Capital Preferred Stock Financings and the NVCA*, Chapters 11–15 walk through the process of actually selling shares, focusing primarily on *valuation*—what that means, the role it plays, and some strategies used to try to get a good one.

In Chapter 16, we talk about the dotcom era and how founders and investors alike couldn't hitch up when they couldn't agree on valuation.

In Chapters 17–24, we do some historical sleuthing, and uncover the solution that the parties hit upon—*convertible seed notes*—and the basic attributes and elements of these investment instruments.

Ten years ago, we might have ended this book there, but given the emergence of a third form of seed deal structure—*the SAFE*—we need to spill more ink.

We cover the SAFE itself in Chapters 36–40, but to lay a strong foundation for that discussion, we plow through the basics of *equity compensation* in Chapters 25–35. By focusing on *restricted shares, stock options, and warrants* in those chapters, we not only create a foundation for the better understanding of SAFEs, but we develop a deep understanding of those other highly relevant portions of the cap table.

Not to be overlooked, we tuck in a sidebar on *Dilution and Pro Rata Rights* between Chapters 20 and 21, and another on the *Contribution of Intellectual Property* between Chapters 27 and 28. And we finish this book with a sidebar on *Securities Laws.*

Whew.

* * *

Every rule, every directive, every principle, every *mild suggestion* laid out in this book—each and every one of them—has been violated or disregarded by a client of mine. Some more than others!

Sometimes they got lucky. Most times, not so much. Now, to be clear, the consequence is not jail (at least not usually . . .). Rather, it's just a sticky situation that takes an emotional toll—along with lots of legal fees that could have been avoided.

Don't be that person, whether as a founder, an entrepreneur, or a legal advisor. It's so easy to do these things properly, especially if you know what the heck the issues are, and what the terminology all means. That's the purpose of this book. To arm you with the knowledge you need to do things right the first time.

* * *

Finally, what the heck is a "seed deal"?

Good question!

If you have picked up this book, there is a good chance that you have heard of something called a "Series A" deal. That's traditional shorthand for a company's first venture capital financing. It carries that designation because the type of shares sold in that financing are called "Series A Preferred Stock." So a "seed deal" is any financing which takes place before the Series A.

Why "seed"? Because this is the "seed stage," the stage at which the earliest cash seeds are planted in the startup garden. Venture capitalists don't invest in seeds. They invest in green shoots. But there are no green shoots without seeds. So learning all about venture capital financings is cool and important, but it means nothing if a startup doesn't attract and secure seed funding first.

And that's what this book is about.

So with that in mind, let's get to it, but first a final word—you can do this startup thing. You really can. And if I can be of any further assistance, please don't hesitate to reach out. I respect you and your struggle. This book is my contribution to the cause. I hope it makes things easier by demystifying and unpacking a lot of these dense and scary topics. But my contribution to your particular cause need not end here. Let me know if I can help:

David@SeedDeals.net

1

The Balance Sheet

I like to start with a balance sheet. For the uninitiated, this is what a balance sheet looks like:

You know what "assets" are. Loosely put, they're all the good stuff in the business—cash, accounts receivable, intellectual property, technology, and so on.

And you know what "liabilities" are. The bad stuff—what's owed the bank, the landlord, the contractors, (the lawyer).

A balance sheet must, well, balance. Expressed mathematically:

$$A = L + E$$

Or, through the power of elementary school math (or college math, if you aren't so STEMmy):

$$A - L = E$$

The good stuff, minus the bad stuff, equals "equity."

Ok, so what? Well, the "so what" is this—equity is where the founder lives!

Put very simply, startups aren't monetized until the end. Startups are concerned with product development over revenues, market share over profitability, and so on.

Yes, there is the relatively rare case where a tech or life science company achieves profitability and throws off cash along the way—but not often. And yes, there is also the occasional IPO (initial public offering), where a company registers its shares with the SEC and offers them to the public—which gives the owners the chance to sell their shares to new investors and make money that way.

For the VAST majority of startups, the "end" is what is sometimes called a liquidity event, or an exit transaction. It's the sale of the company. Another company buys the startup.

There are many different forms of "M&A" transactions (which means mergers and acquisitions). Lots of ways these deals can be structured. But at the most basic level, when a startup is sold, its assets are turned into cash.

So all that good stuff the startup created and built over the years gets converted into cash. Those are the "gross proceeds"—the total amount collected. From the gross proceeds, the startup pays off its liabilities—all those debts and payables, all that bad stuff that's accumulated on the balance sheet.

Whatever is left over goes to equity. Those leftovers are sometimes called the "net proceeds."

From a jargon perspective, this process is sometimes called the "waterfall." Why? Because the cash "flows" down:

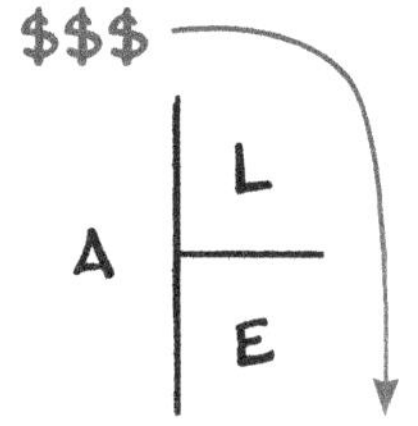

Get it? Pay off the liabilities first, in their proper order. And not just because it's the nice thing to do—it's a legal requirement (best to avoid orange jumpsuits whenever possible!). Whatever is left over flows down to equity. It's why these are called liquidity events. The cash flows like liquid. Like a waterfall. Whoosh.

2

The Cap Table (Ownership Percentages)

So now we know what a balance sheet is. We know what an exit is, and why it's important. And we know that the balance sheet and the exit connect. The assets convert into cash, which flows vertically down the right side of the balance sheet, paying off the liabilities and then pooling in equity.

And equity, well, that belongs to the owners!

Regardless of whether you know how to swim or have an affinity for chlorine, know this—startups want to create an ocean of equity, not a mere puddle. And they get that by creating and then selling lots of valuable assets while only generating and carrying relatively few liabilities.

Ok, great, so the startup accomplished that—well done! It did everything it set out to do. Built something amazing, sold it, and now the startup has cash for days. a big equity pool. Splash.

What comes next?

Well, naturally, we need to divvy that cash up. Who gets it?

This is the part of the movie where the bank robbers meet in the hideout after the heist and split up the gains. And you know how someone always ends up getting WAY less than they expected? That's why I wrote this book, and that's why you are reading it. We don't want that to happen here.

The founder should not be the sucker or the mark. No way. Not on my watch.

This is where the "capitalization table"—or cap table, for short—comes in. Yeah, I know, thinking about briefcases full of cash is more fun . . .

Ok, so back to the cap table. What's that? Well, it tells you who gets what. And the "who" in that sentence is the owners.

Let's start with a simple cap table:

	SHARES	%	
A			
B			
C			
		100%	

This startup has three founders. And, remarkably, they are named Founder A, Founder B, and Founder C (they were fated to work together).

When I sit with a team for the first time, I ask them to explain their ownership structure to me—in other words, we start with that righthand column. I want to know, on a percentage basis, how much each founder owns. And the results are often interesting.

Founder A says, "Well, it's my idea, I'm doing this full-time, and I'm the CEO. As the three of us have discussed, I own 70%."

Founder B says, "Well, I'm the tech co-founder. We know how critical my role is. And as we discussed, I own 40%."

Founder C says, "Well, that's all well and good, but I do marketing and sales and all that, and without me, this is just a science-fair project—so as we discussed, I own 40%."

You can do the math. We all like to think we give 150% all day, every day, right?

But spreadsheets don't like that. You get my point. The ownership percentages must add up to 100%. Always.

The initial allocation of ownership among the founders is tough. There is no obvious default position. In our hypo, it could be 1/3 for each—or it could be 98/1/1. Every company is a snowflake, and these conversations often devolve into debates and then disintegrate into fights. Try to avoid that.

It's often said that you know you've struck a good deal when everyone feels a little frustrated and a little put-upon, but no one is furious or bloodthirsty. That principle most certainly applies here.

So ok, our three founders went back to the drawing board and worked it out. Our cap table now looks like this:

	SHARES	%	
A		60%	
B		30%	
C		10%	
		100%	

Now we're cooking with gas!

3

The Cap Table (Shares)

Before taking the next step, let's remind ourselves why we are so focused on getting the ownership percentages right.

Founders pour their very LIVES into their startup. It's all-consuming, for all the right reasons—as we discussed at the jump. But founders also want to cash a check when it's all said and done.

To do so, the startup must be sold. All that good stuff, all those assets, needs to get converted into cash.

Then working through the waterfall, the liabilities get paid-off.

What's left is for equity—and it's a lot. Nice!

The question is, how do we allocate that equity in a manner that doesn't involve gladiatorial battles or cage matches? That's where the cap table comes in. The cap table tells us what to do. How? Because those ownership percentages directly express how much of the equity pool—how much of the net proceeds from the exit transaction—each owner gets. That's pretty important!

Look how far we have already come. Boom.

So what's next? Well, you'll notice that our cap table has two columns. We've played with one—ownership percentages. The other is labeled "shares."

Shares embody ownership interests. Sometimes, in partnerships especially, shares aren't used at all. The partners simply maintain a ledger which shows ownership percentages. One column.

But that's not the norm. It's simply easier to track ownership by using something tangible. Our minds work better that way. When we gathered nuts and berries on the savannah tens of thousands of years ago, we knew at a glance what we had—what we owned. We are still gathering nuts and berries. We just call them shares (and when we get deeper into this book, and start selling shares, you'll really see the benefit and convenience of this system).

If your company is a limited liability company (an LLC), these might be called membership interests, units, or shares. Or something else. The label doesn't really matter. What's represented is what matters. With a corporation, these are called shares, or shares of stock. But regardless, what we are talking about are ownership interests—in other words, the literal claim on equity. It's an IOU of sorts, written from the company to its owners.

So the shares represent ownership, and they, of course, must tie out to the percentages. Sometimes at this stage, you'll hear these shares referenced as "founder shares," because, well, they are shares issued to founders. See, not everything is hard!

So back to our cap table:

	SHARES	%	
A	6	60%	
B	3	30%	
C	1	10%	
	10	100%	

The math works. For instance, for Founder A, 6 / 10 = 60%. Or we could have done this:

	SHARES	%	
A	6M	60%	
B	3M	30%	
C	1M	10%	
	10M	100%	

Any difference? Not economically. 6M / 10M = 60%.

The point is this—it's RELATIVE. And here's what's funny. When a founder holds six shares of stock in a startup, her friends think she has lost her mind. "Six shares?!? That's nothing! I own 12 shares in GE. That's not worth that much—but it's worth twice as much as what you have! Dummy!"

That reaction is so typical as to be almost universal. But it's riddled with misconceptions. Let's unpack it.

A basic equation:

$$\frac{\text{VALUATION}}{\text{TOTAL SHARES}} = \text{PRICE PER SHARE (PPS)}$$

[OR FLIPPED]

$$\text{TOTAL SHARES} \times \text{PPS} = \text{VALUATION}$$

Let's say that GE is trading at $10/share. And let's say there are 9,000,000,000 shares outstanding. That means GE is worth $90,000,000,000.

Based on that information, the friend's 12 shares are worth a total of $120. And her ownership percentage of GE is infinitesimally small—namely, 12 / 9,000,000,000 = 0.00000013%.

You know what this means. If GE sells all its assets and pays off its liabilities and has money to spare, that money—equity—goes to the owners. And the friend will get a tinyyyyyyyyyy taste of it.

Now let's consider the startup. Yes, the founder "only" holds six shares, but those six shares represent a total ownership of 60% of the company. Pretty sure that's worth more than $120—even on day 1. And (hopefully) it only goes up from there.

Of course, the friend would have been a lot more impressed, and no one would have needed a calculator, if the founder had said, "Hey gang, guess what? I own 6,000,000 shares of my startup." The reaction? "Nice. #Baller. You are buying drinks."

They still don't get it. Six million shares don't make the founder a baller any more than six shares make the founder a dummy. The numbers themselves don't matter. It's only relative.

Our brains have been wired differently because we spend our lives exposed to the big companies who are traded on the big stock exchanges, where the total share numbers and total valuations are massive, and share prices tend to range from $10 to $100. The companies manipulate their share numbers to work that way.

So that's the mental math we do—a share is worth that much, period. So when we hear six shares, we typically assume those shares have a total value somewhere between $60 and $600.

And to be fair, that may make sense as a shorthand in the stock exchange slice of the world. But it doesn't in Startupland.

But THAT being said—that doesn't mean we ignore those reactions, discount them, or spend our lives evangelizing to the contrary (I've tried; I've given up; let it go). Instead, like a martial arts expert, we take that punch, reverse its energy, and use it for our own purposes, to our advantage.

We know that shares only matter on a relative basis—relative, that is, to the total number of shares outstanding. But we'll go ahead and use big numbers, simply because it takes the dumb reactions from friends off the table. Or maybe—if we are being honest—even our own dumb reactions.

So we'll give the founder 6,000,000 shares. Friends will be impressed. That's cool. But it may mean picking up more tabs at the bar.

One side note before we continue. If you are a tech or life science startup, it's likely that you formed your company as a corporation and did so in the state of Delaware. There are several very good reasons for that, but the bottom line is that Delaware corporations—and even more specifically, Delaware "C" corporations (that "C" is a tax designation under the Internal Revenue Code)—are the customary choice-of-entity for tech and life science startups.

The document by which the corporation is actually created is called a "Certificate of Incorporation." In that document, we "authorize" the maximum number of shares the company may issue (don't worry; it's easy to increase later). We are then asked to give these shares a "par value." That's an old-timey concept with little meaning now. It's like a spleen.

It's so meaningless, in fact, that many states allow you to authorize shares "without par value"—including Delaware. But if you are a Delaware corporation—DO NOT fall into this trap. Give your shares a low par value. I typically use $0.00001. Don't worry—this has nothing to do with the "value" of your company (more on that topic below, when we get into valuation).

The reason you want to assign shares a par value is this: the companies need to pay Delaware an annual "franchise tax" for the privilege of using their brand. Delaware will send a bill which calculates that tax based on the number of shares authorized. If the company has authorized 10,000,000 shares (as our example would require), its tax will be tens of thousands of dollars. Say what?!?

But don't fret—if the shares have a par value, you can use a different methodology based on net assets. As a tech or life science startup, net assets will be low, and likely will be for many years. Under that methodology, the tax will be measured merely in the hundreds of dollars. Whew.

But that alternative is NOT available if the shares have no par value.

This is a crazy technical point, and it feels out of place in a big picture book like this, but because of the cash liability swing, it's of massive importance and relevance to startups and founders. Please take note.

Ok, take a breath. Glad we got that out of the way. Let's move on and get back into it.

CHOICE-OF-ENTITY AND DELAWARE "C" CORPORATIONS

A quick side note on choice-of-entity analysis and Delaware "C" corporations. If this book is already big picture, this portion will be biiiiiiiiiig picture. But still, it's an important enough topic that a few words are necessary just to level-set.

Sole proprietorships and general partnerships are easy to form. The participants just act. No filing necessary. Yay!

But the owners have unlimited liability for the debts and obligations of the business. Boo!

Corporations and LLCs offer what's called "limited liability" protection to their owners, meaning that the owners can lose what they literally invested, but the rest of their assets are insulated from the debts and obligations of the entity. Yay!

Now, tax. Partnerships offer "pass-through" taxation, which means that the company itself does not pay tax on gains (or take the losses)—it "passes them through" to the owners. So gains are taxed only once (at the owner level), and losses can (often) be taken by the owners personally to offset gains from other income, which is a nice benefit.

"C" corporations don't get this benefit. Losses remain in the entity, and gains are taxed at the entity level—and then if subsequent distributions are made to the owners, these are (generally) taxed as well. This is so-called "double taxation."

LLCs often elect to be taxed as partnerships. When they do, you'll sometimes see them referred to as LLC-Ps.

"S" corporations (another tax designation you may have heard of) are a lot like partnerships, but there are several downsides, including limitations on the number of owners (cannot exceed 100), the type of owners (generally just humans), and the types of shares they can sell (only one type allowed; more on why this matters in the chapters that follow). They just don't work well for tech and life science startups.

So if we are dealing with a tech or life science startup, it seems obvious, no? An LLC-P! Why organize as a "C" corporation and suffer double taxation? Seems crazy. I mean, we all want to do our part as good citizens, but still . . .

But if you are reading this book, you've likely heard that, in Startupland, the "C" corporation—in particular, the Delaware "C" corporation—is the preferred form. But why?

Well, for one thing, "C" corporations can take advantage of Section 1202 of the Internal Revenue Code (IRC). I try to limit tax talk where I can in this book, but sometimes it's important, and this is one of those places. Section 1202 addresses something called "Qualified Small Business Stock," or QSBS. It's a bit technical, but the bottom line is that for founders, the stock they are issued almost always qualifies, and if the founders hold that stock for at least five years, the founders will (generally) pay no tax on the gain. Wow!

Exactly. Wow! And Section 1202 does not apply to LLCs.

Further lessening the "C" corporation blow, buyers of startups (those big whales who will buy the company in a liquidity event or exit transaction) are accustomed to buying "C" corporations. There are provisions of the IRC that they frequently will take advantage of which lessen or even sometimes eliminate the pain of double taxation. An example would be something called "tax-free reorganizations." These provisions are not applicable to LLCs.

Finally, traditional venture capital investors have a strong aversion to pass-through entities. Their tax-exempt investors don't want something called "unrelated business taxable income" (UBTI), and their foreign investors don't want to get swept into the US tax regime. Both are a greater risk with pass-through entities than with "C" corporations. (Plus, to be frank, the day-to-day administration of LLC-Ps is a hassle. "C" corporations are just easier.)

Ok, so that explains "C" corporations. What's this Delaware stuff?

As a general matter, corporate law in the US resides at the state level. There really isn't "federal" corporate law.

For a variety of reasons—history, tradition, custom, practice, highly-evolved statutes, responsive agencies, sophisticated courts, and so on—Delaware has emerged as the premier home for tech and life science startups (and many other types of corporations, to be sure).

So what most startups do is incorporate in Delaware, forming themselves as a Delaware corporation. They elect to be taxed as a "C" corporation under the IRC. And then they file a simple form with the state in which they actually reside or operate, "qualifying" themselves to do business there.

Easy peasy!

4

Types of Shares

You know how there are types of liabilities? Bank debt is different from employee wages is different from rent is different from what is owed the lawyer (there it is again; sorry about my tick . . .).

Same holds true of equity. The first difference you need to understand is the difference between types of shares.

There are 2 types of shares—common shares and preferred shares.

Before we jump into the details and compare and contrast the two, let me make a single point which cannot be emphasized strongly enough: *Common shares and preferred shares are (generally) interchangeable on a one-to-one basis (1:1). One share (generally) equals one vote, and far more importantly, one share (generally) relates to the same percentage of ownership.*

Why the emphasis on this point? Because founders and investors alike spend enormous energy hand-wringing over the details of preferred shares and deal terms generally. Heck, that's what a lot of this book is about! And that's fine. But don't miss the forest for the trees.

So much of these negotiations take place on the edges—skirmishes over minor, ancillary points. Try not to get wrapped around those axles. Existentially, these shares represent the same thing.

The same thing!

Ok, with that off my chest, moving on.

5

Common Shares

As a general matter, anyone who gets their shares for SERVICES gets common shares. Executives, employees, directors, consultants—and founders. There are exceptions, but they are rare, and they tend to make the cap table look amateurish. So I suggest sticking to the norm. Common.

This is the proverbial "sweat equity." See, sometimes the terminology really does speak for itself!

Founders sometimes like to get a little fancy with common shares. They may create 2 classes of common—one voting and one non-voting. They get the voting shares, and everyone else gets non-voting shares.

But to be honest? It rarely has much meaning. It would be an unusual cap table in the tech or life science world where the votes of non-founder common stockholders could actually change the outcome. But if the founder is adamant, I won't stand in the way.

In recent years, a trend toward "super-voting" shares has emerged. It's where founders give themselves special common shares with more than one vote per share. It's usually set at 5–10 votes per share. Going above that ratio can start to look a little suspect, so don't do it.

Founders need to be careful with super-voting shares. They can signal that the founder is a control freak who is not open to feedback and cares little about good governance. And why do super-voting shares signal that? Because it's often true . . .

I'm not saying don't do it. I'm just saying that if you do it, think long and hard about it and be prepared for some pushback.

But that's about it on common shares. You can play around with voting rights and voting ratios, but economically, they are all the same.

On the other hand, preferred shares . . .

6

Preferred Shares

Anyone who gets their shares for SERVICES gets common shares. In contrast, anyone who gets their shares for MONEY gets preferred shares. Why? Well, if given the choice between something called "common" and something called "preferred," wouldn't you . . . (here it comes) . . . *prefer* the latter?

If common shares basically are what they are, with some limited opportunity for tweaking on the edges, preferred shares are infinitely malleable.

But that's not helpful. So let's break it down. At a high level, most preferred shares are endowed with special control rights and with special economic rights.

7

Preferred Shares (Control)

Wow, that was quick.

You're welcome!

From time to time, allowing yourself mini-accomplishments is quite gratifying. So—nice job blazing through Chapter 6 so quickly!

Ok, getting into it:

For preferred shareholders, control shows up in two ways.

First, preferred shareholders ask for something they call "protective provisions." Founders call these "blocking rights" or "veto rights." Some lawyers and bankers refer to them as "negative covenants."

What are they? Well, these are things that the company cannot do without the approval of some percentage of the preferred shareholders (usually a majority, measured by the number of preferred shares outstanding—sometimes referred to as a "majority-in-interest"). They always include big-ticket items like sale of the company, distributing cash to shareholders, or selling more shares. They sometimes include next-level matters like taking on debt, fundamentally changing the business model, or changing the number of directors on the Board. They occasionally get into more day-to-day matters like approving the budget, hiring executives, or paying compensation in excess of a certain amount to any employee.

Note that these rights only give preferred shareholders the opportunity to BLOCK an action. They do not provide preferred shareholders with the right to INITIATE these actions on their own.

What does that mean? Well, for instance, the Board can recommend that the company sell more shares, but the preferred shareholders can vote no. But the preferred shareholders cannot themselves initiate the transaction and force the company to go and sell those shares. That's the difference between a negative covenant and an affirmative covenant. And these are the former and not the latter.

Ok, so that's that for protective provisions. I said two control rights. What's the other?

A Board seat.

Shareholders have very few voting rights under law. But wait, what about protective provisions? Those are not required by law. Think of them as negotiated between the parties, like a contract.

One of the things that shareholders do vote on are directors—they elect the members of the company's Board of Directors.

The Board of Directors manages the affairs of the company. They elect and oversee the company's officers, who run the day-to-day, and they have general responsibility for setting the strategy and tone of the company's overall direction and trajectory.

In other words, directors have a lot of responsibility and access to a lot of information about the company. Shareholders have neither. So preferred shareholders often negotiate for the right to designate one or more members of the Board.

Note that preferred shareholders rarely have the right to "control" the Board—meaning that they cannot designate a majority of the directors. If a potential investor asks for that, that should raise a red flag. It suggests a lack of sophistication—or a hankering for profound control bordering on the sociopathic. Neither is attractive.

Founders often get prickly about the constitution and composition of the Board. And not unreasonably. Note one point I made above—directors elect and oversee the company's officers.

Being a "founder" is not a job. It's an existential role—which is not an insult. If anything, it's a compliment. It highlights the leap taken, the pressure endured, the commitment made. Like a double helix, the founder's soul and that of the startup are intertwined.

But back to earth. It's not a "job" per se. The founder is "Founder and CEO." Or "Founder and CTO." Or whatever. In other words, the founder is an officer, with duties and responsibilities. And the founder has a boss. The Board.

The officers report to the Board. And the Board manages the officers. And the Board can fire them. That is why founders are touchy about the Board. And rightfully so.

And that is why preferred shareholders, in the vast majority of cases, do NOT ask for majority control of the Board. They understand how radioactive such a request would be.

But they do usually ask for—and get—some representation in the boardroom, and that's ok. They want access to information and, even more importantly, the opportunity to listen to the conversation and influence it. Frankly, this is the kind of input and participation that should be welcomed. It will make the startup better.

8

Preferred Shares (Economics)

Remember our earlier discussion of the waterfall? Double-click on that mental file folder.

To recap (or re-cap, heh), here's a balance sheet:

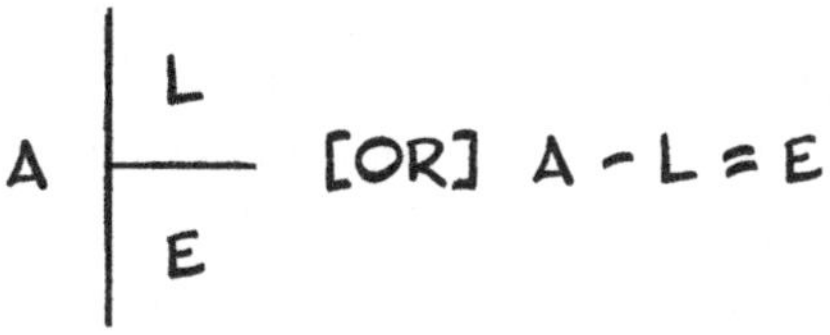

Most people think "liquidation" is a bad thing. Teenagers wearing placards outside a store declaring "Going out of Business! Liquidation! 90% Off! Everything Must Go!"

And yeah, that's a type of liquidation. But if a startup sells its assets for $5,000,000,000 and pays off $100,000,000 in liabilities, leaving $4,900,000,000—well, to get that boatload of cash into the hands of shareholders, the company must be "liquidated." No placards or teenagers required.

When the startup is sold and its assets liquified into cash, the liabilities are then paid off. What's left—the net proceeds—is available for equity. To shake those net proceeds free, to crack open that company egg and drop that yolk to the shareholders, we **LIQUIDATE** the company.

But here's the punchline—preferred shareholders have certain economic rights in liquidation that common shareholders (including founders) do not have.

There is something called a "liquidation preference." This is a multiple of the preferred shareholder's purchase price. So if the preferred shareholder paid $1.00/share, its liquidation preference is "X" times $1.00.

Almost always, the multiple is 1. So the preferred shares will carry a 1X liquidation preference—here, $1.00. By the way, if it's not 1, ask some questions. There are rare cases where a higher multiple (it's never lower) is appropriate—but those are highly circumstantial and one-offs. Like in the case of an investor seeking majority control of the Board, your sociopath radar may rightly ping here.

Ok, fine, liquidation preference. So what?

The "so what" requires that we look at something called "participation." Specifically, there are two types of preferred shares: "non-participating" and "participating."

But before we jump in to those waters, a quick word on dividends.

Throughout this book, we make occasional reference to "Main Street companies," meaning those businesses who strive to monetize their assets through ongoing profitability (rather than focusing exclusively on exit). The typical means by which these companies distribute this excess cash to shareholders is by way of a cash dividend.

Tech and life science companies, in contrast, tend not to find themselves in the position of having excess cash. So the declaration of cash dividends is not really a thing they do.

Nonetheless, in close proximity to the description of preferred shares as non-participating or participating, you will often see dividends specifically referenced. And referenced similarly as, well, non-cumulative or cumulative. Non-participating preferred tends to travel with non-cumulative dividends, and participating preferred tends to travel with cumulative dividends. It doesn't have to work that way; it can be vice versa. But this is the norm.

Non-cumulative dividends (sometimes called "non-accruing dividends") require that they be literally "declared" by the company's Board of Directors to be triggered. This is extraordinarily rare in Startupland,

and so non-cumulative dividends can be largely ignored. They arise in edge hypotheticals and outlier scenarios only.

Cumulative dividends, on the other hand, are meaningful. They act like interest, and automatically accrue. They are typically calculated as a percentage of the share purchase price. They could be lower than 5%, or higher than 20%, but in the vast majority of deals, it's 8% (maybe toggling as low as 6% or as high as 10%). Are they paid along the way? Rarely. So what's the deal?

Bottom line—cumulative dividends (sometimes called "accruing dividends") are added to the liquidation preference. We'll see the manner in which this plays out below. But the impact can be meaningful.

If the preferred shares were purchased at $1.00/share, and if they carry an 8% cumulative dividend, then that's $0.08 per year. If the shares are held for, say, five years, then that means that the total accrued dividends sum out to $0.40 per share—that's a 40% return on invested capital. At scale, this matters. If the startup has raised $10,000,000 in preferred shares with cumulative dividends, then the total liquidation preference is not merely $10,000,000 (or 1X)—it's $14,000,000. Maybe not gamechanging, but it's not chicken scratch, either.

9

Non-Participating Preferred Shares

Non-participating preferred shares are signaled by the conjunction "or." At liquidation, non-participating preferred shareholders get the greater of (1) their liquidation preference, OR (2) their ownership percentage of the net proceeds.

It's what people sometimes call "downside protection." The company has a boatload of cash to distribute? Then it's door #2, and non-participating preferred looks just like common. But if things go badly, and scratching together net proceeds is like flipping over sofa cushions looking for pizza money, then it's door #1, and things look very different for common.

How about a quick example, you ask? Sure!

Let's say the company has one preferred shareholder who paid $1.00/share for 1,000,000 preferred shares, which represent an ownership interest of 20%. That's a total liquidation preference of $1,000,000.

And if that preferred shareholder owns 20% of the startup, then that means the founding group owns 80%.

If the company sells, and the net proceeds total $200,000,000, then the preferred shareholder will get the greater of $1,000,000 (its liquidation preference) or $40,000,000 (20% of the total). It will take the latter. Um, duh. Plays just like common, side-by-side. It gets $40,000,000, and the founding group gets $160,000,000, and everyone is drunkenly happy.

But what if the company sells and the net proceeds total \$2,000,000? Then the preferred shareholder will get the greater of \$1,000,000 (its liquidation preference) or \$400,000 (20% of the total). In that case, it will take the former. Um, duh.

Framed a bit differently, our waterfall (written sideways) would look like this:

$$A - L - LP = E$$

LP MEANING "LIQUIDATION PREFERENCE"

Now remember it's an "or." Once the preferred shareholder collects its liquidation preference, it's off the board.

So in our example, if there are net proceeds of \$2,000,000, that must mean this:

$$A - L = \$2,000,000$$

That's the basic definition of net proceeds: assets minus liabilities.

But if we flow through the waterfall and scrape-off the liquidation preference before sending the balance to equity, our math looks like this:

$$A - L - LP = E, \text{ SO}$$

$$\$2,000,000 - \$1,000,000 = \$1,000,000$$

Which means there is \$1,000,000 available for the founding group. Which is where founders get confused.

Our example has the preferred shareholder at 20%. Which means our founding group is at 80%. If they hear that the net proceeds are \$2,000,000, they may be logically thinking that they get 80% of that, or \$1,600,000. But instead, because the non-participating preferred shares first get the benefit of the liquidation preference, the founding group only gets \$1,000,000 (the "net net" proceeds, or what's left after the \$1,000,000 liquidation preference is paid). They get 100% of that \$1,000,000 because the preferred shareholder is off the board, but still . . .

It's better than a sharp stick in the eye, but definitely a disappointment.

Many founders say this is "unfair." Investors counter by saying, look, what's not fair is returning $400,000 to me on a $1,000,000 investment. I did my part by writing you a check. Getting my money back before you get anything is entirely "fair" under these bad circumstances.

As you well know (or will most certainly learn), any time someone uses the word "fair" in a negotiation or debate, you know they are scraping the bottom of the argumentation barrel. It's not a strong comeback. It sounds weak and a little whiny. Playgroundish.

Same here. These economic terms—and their application—are neither fair nor unfair to investors or to founders. It's just economics. It's negotiated. It's the playing field. These are not windmills at which to tilt. These are simply deal points to understand and to prepare for accordingly.

But while we are on the topic of fairness . . .

10

Participating Preferred Shares

If non-participating preferred shares are characterized by the word "or," then, perhaps not surprisingly, participating preferred shares are defined by the use of the word "and."

There is no "greater of" decision-tree. It's not liquidation preference OR ownership percentage of the net proceeds. It's AND. It's both. Always.

So in our example above, the total liquidation preference is $1,000,000, and the ownership percentage is 20%. And note that if these preferred shares also carried an 8% cumulative dividend, and if these shares were held for five years, then the total liquidation preference would be $1,400,000 ($1,000,000 plus $400,000 in total accrued dividends).

Whether the net proceeds are $200,000,000 or $2,000,000, that liquidation preference is always scraped-off first (paid to the preferred shareholder)—and then that preferred shareholder STILL gets 20% of what's left.

Founders sometimes call this "double-dipping." Investors sometimes call this "appropriate compensation for the risk taken in backing a highly speculative early-stage startup." But again, however characterized, try to avoid thinking about this in terms of "fairness." It will get you nowhere. Instead, seek to understand.

In the tech and life science startup world, preferred shares are market. That's what is sold to investors, period. Where there is room to negotiate is whether those preferred shares are non-participating or participating. That's fair game.

Most founders don't have too much trouble with non-participating preferred shares. They don't like it, to be sure, but the logic as laid-out above does hold some water. But participating preferred is a different kettle of fish altogether.

I encourage you to think of it this way: investors want a return. In Startupland, usually 5X-10X. Which means they want their $1,000,000 turned into $5,000,000–$10,000,000. Ownership percentage is one place where this gets negotiated. How much of the company does an investor need to own to tee-up that kind of return opportunity? That conversation dominates the next portion of this book, starting in the next chapter.

But another way for an investor to get there, or at least to improve its chances, is by asking for participating preferred (and perhaps cumulative dividends as well). If it isn't completely satisfied with its ownership percentage—or if it simply wants to hedge its risk just a bit more—the investor may ask for this economic right. Unlike some of the other deal points mentioned earlier, seeking this right does not make it a sociopath—or even make the investor "unfair." It's a calculation and should simply be treated as such.

All that said, as a general matter, non-participating preferred is more prevalent than participating preferred in the startup marketplace. Why? Investors may concede some economics by not pushing for the latter, but in exchange, they are better aligned with the founders, and perhaps even more importantly at the seed stage, they set a tone.

A tone?

There is something called "stacking" in the biz, which refers to the piling of liquidation preference on liquidation preference. A seed investor may negotiate for, and get, participating preferred for its $500,000 investment, and proudly pat itself on the back. But that increases the likelihood that future investors will, too, insist on participating preferred—that's the "tone." So if this seed investor ultimately finds itself buried under $50M of future liquidation preferences—well, did they really "win"?

In other words, participating preferred can bite a seed investor every bit as hard as a founder.

Nevertheless, there are investors who insist on participating preferred, especially in tough economic times, as a way to mitigate risk and enhance upside.

There are some who take the philosophical position that founders should reject participating preferred always and every time. I certainly would agree that non-participating preferred is to be, well, *preferred* by founders. But my position on the question is less ideological and more pragmatic.

Even if the founder fails in her efforts to write participating preferred out of the deal, if she still likes the rest of the deal, and if she still likes the investor, then she should do the deal. Plenty of founders have made a lot of money in startups with participating preferred shares on the cap table. Plenty.

And sometimes it can be flipped around.

If an investor insists on participating preferred, then perhaps it can be pushed on valuation, and the company can get a higher number. That's not a bad trade—the double-dip isn't great, but with a higher valuation, the founders will hold on to a higher percentage of ownership. That can help rebalance the economics. In other words, conceding on participating preferred is not inevitably catastrophic.

What IS catastrophic is not getting a handle on ownership percentages and how they are calculated and managed in the context of investment transactions themselves. That's where founders truly run the risk of squandering their opportunity, of turning a healthy slice of the pie into a single M&M. It is to that topic we now turn.

VENTURE CAPITAL PREFERRED STOCK FINANCINGS AND THE NVCA

The focus of this book is seed deals. And in the Introduction, I defined a seed deal as any financing which precedes the traditional venture capital "Series A" financing.

This is not a book on venture capital financings. That being said, it's important for you to know, for purposes of context, a few things about those deals. Primarily because it's relevant for your seed deals.

First things first, a "Series A" venture capital financing always involves the sale of preferred shares with the sorts of features we've been discussing. Seed deals can also be structured as the sale of preferred shares—sometimes called "Seed Preferred" or "Series Seed Preferred." But they can take other forms as well, and we'll get to that later in the book.

There is an organization known as the National Venture Capital Association (the NVCA). The NVCA is a trade group which, among other things, hosts a catalog of "Model Legal Documents." These documents are available for free on the website. Free!

The benefit of the model documents is that they have normalized the terms and structure of venture capital financings. This saves lawyers a lot of headaches—and founders and investors a lot of time and money. That's a good thing.

Seed deals don't always follow these terms and structure. But they frequently do. And even when they don't, they anticipate future venture capital financings which will indeed follow these NVCA terms and structure. So directly or indirectly, the NVCA model documents impact seed deals.

There are five key documents which comprise the basic suite. They are: (1) the Certificate of Incorporation, (2) the Stock Purchase Agreement, (3) the Investor Rights Agreement, (4) the Right of First Refusal and Co-Sale Agreement, and (5) the Voting Agreement.

At a high level, the actual preferred shares are created under document #1. Pursuant to document #2, the investor actually buys the preferred shares. And under documents #3–#5, the going-forward rules of the road relating to governance and control are outlined.

In seed deals, you may see these forms used in full. You may see these forms, but see them skinnied down. You may see these forms, but see them skinnied down, and collapsed into fewer documents (for instance, documents #3–#5 may just be rolled into a single "Stockholders Agreement"). Or you may not see these forms at all and instead see taken a wholly different approach to documentation.

Why the variety? While venture capital financings have gotten incredibly standardized and normalized (thank you, NVCA!), seed deals are still highly diverse. Why? Well, start with the fact that you can have $10,000 seed deals or $10,000,000 seed deals. You can have one investor—or 50. You can have a single closing (meaning all the money at once), or 10+ closings. And, as advertised above, you may not even be selling preferred shares.

But even so, in structuring a seed deal, keep one eye keenly looking ahead. The seed deal is a pathway, not an end point. You'll want what you do today to feather into what you do tomorrow.

Ok, that's all well and good, you may say. But what should I look to? How do I know what I need to know?

The most useful document published by the NVCA is the Model Term Sheet.

A term sheet is a non-binding document that appears in most transactions (seed deals included). It can be as simple as a three-line email, or as complex as 25 pages in eight-point font. But the basic objective is to outline the core terms of the deal, in advance, so that the parties have some assurance that they are aligned before they release the lawyers into the wild to draft the definitive binding documents.

The NVCA's Model Term Sheet is special because it includes various deal-point alternatives, which allow you to choose your own adventure. It's also annotated.

If you want a basic primer on venture capital financings, you can find a book on the topic, but I would first recommend that you simply download the Model Term Sheet and work your way through the footnotes. Between this book and that Model Term Sheet, you'll be 97.6%* of the way home!

*Not scientific . . .

11

Selling Shares (Getting Started)

It took some time for us to get here, but here we are—let's go raise some money!

At this point, the startup has done a lot of things right. Company launched. Hacked together a minimum viable product (an MVP) or got traction in the lab. Maybe even closed some sales or partnerships, or filed a few patent applications. Off to the races!

But taking the next step requires more money than it's got. It's time to go fundraise.

You sometimes hear the descriptor "FFFs" used for investors at this stage. It means friends, family, and fools. One and two are fine. Let's avoid the third.

The first two categories are logical—these are people who know and like the founder, and who are betting specifically on the founder. Not the concept, not the product-market fit, not the technology—the human. Virtually every startup gets its start through capital invested by friends and family.

A warning however—going into business with family is always tricky. Make sure these people can afford to lose it all. Make sure that they are patient and don't need the money. Make sure they don't think this makes them "one of the team" in the sense that now they get to show up whenever they want . . . and offer to "help."

But a further warning—they shouldn't be taken advantage of either. Provide complete disclosure. Don't mislead. And don't pitch terms which aren't market. More on that below.

As for fools, no. In fact, what you want are anti-fools. You want experts. Specifically, people who have been there/done that in adjacent companies and industries (and who have some disposable income). These are the best proverbial "angel investors."

They can write the check, and they are easier to sell because they "get it" immediately. They don't have to be persuaded that "here's a problem, here's how we solve it, and here are the likely customers." They get one minute into the conversation, their eyes light up, and they say, yeah, that's right—we had that issue, we never could find a fix, this is great!

Quick sidebar on fundraising—whether raising the first $10,000 or the last $10,000,000, there is one transcendent principle: every contact must become a node and not a terminal point.

As early as the first meeting with a potential investor, politely and with finesse, the founder should ask that prospect if they can think of one or two other people who might be interested. Or who might know someone who might be interested. All this particular prospective investor has to do is forward the proverbial "forwardable email" to its contact and make the connection. As simple as that!

Fundraising is a numbers game. It requires networking on steroids. There is nothing linear about it. Serendipity—the basic good fortune of just finally bouncing into your love connection—is ultimately what's required. And while a founder cannot make serendipity happen, she can most certainly improve her chances.

How? By simply meeting and pitching as many people as possible—by growing the network. And the network grows through introductions.

A "no" to a pitch is ok—founders grow thick skin and get used to it. What's not ok is to have the path dead-end there. Take the "no" (or maybe the "yes"!), and then ask to be linked to someone else.

Create lots of nodes. Avoid terminal points.

12

Selling Shares (Actually Doing It)

So let's say that "yes" has been secured. Whether friend or family or anti-fool, the founder has locked-in the startup's first investor, let's say for $50,000. Congratulations! But now what?

Before we go there, let's take a beat. What the founder has just accomplished is something incredibly important and meaningful. Another human has been persuaded that the startup is up to something interesting, valuable, and worth investing in. This investor likes the team, likes the product, likes the market—likes everything about it. And they have even reached agreement on the actual amount of the investment!

While the founder is busy building the startup, life is happening, too. It doesn't pause and it doesn't wait. Founders owe it to themselves—to their hearts, to their souls, to their emotional well-being—to acknowledge the accomplishments along the way. And to give themselves some credit for these wins.

Startupland is ruggedly mountainous territory with limited rainfall and poor soil. It's hard out here on these streets (forgive my town-and-country mixed metaphors). So take a moment for congratulations. This is not the end—the founder has not yet created and converted a massive pot of assets into a massive pile of cash. But it's a great start!

Alrighty then. Bottle popped and bottle consumed. Back to it. We need to sell these shares and formally wrap this up.

In all likelihood, what we are selling are preferred shares. We know there are a variety of terms that we'll need to sort through, but the fundamental question is the most important one: namely, how many shares does the investor get?

You know why this is important. We need to know the number of shares so that we can calculate for this investor—along with everyone else (including the founders)—what ownership percentage is held by each. And we need to know that so that each person knows what would be their allocation of net proceeds in an exit event. Transparency and certainty are essential.

Fine and dandy. So how do we do this? There are two interrelated equations, and you've already seen one. Let's lay them out and then dive in:

$$\frac{\text{VALUATION}}{\text{TOTAL SHARES}} = \text{PRICE PER SHARE (PPS)}$$

[AND]

$$\frac{\text{INVESTMENT AMOUNT}}{\text{PPS}} = \text{\# OF SHARES SOLD}$$

Let's go bottom up. We know the "Investment Amount"—it's $50,000. But we don't know the "Price per Share." That's ok, because the first equation tells us how to calculate that. And recall we saw this equation way earlier in the book, when we were trying to explain why holding six shares in a startup really is clutch (but then we gave up on that and just decided to make it 6,000,000 shares because, well, why not. Baller.).

The input for the denominator—"Total Shares"—is the total shares outstanding right now, before the investment is made. Sometimes this is called "pre-money"—it's BEFORE the (new) MONEY.

Using the example from the top of this book, and which we'll revisit in more detail shortly, the total count of pre-money shares is 10,000,000. Noted. So what about the numerator? What about "Valuation"?

Well, my friend, this is where it really gets interesting.

13

Valuation

First things first, we are talking once again about "pre-money." We are endeavoring to determine the "pre-money valuation" of the startup. That's just the kind of jargon that you've probably already been exposed to and which has left you feeling unequipped to negotiate in this arena. Let's fix that!

Bottom line—what is the startup worth today, before taking on that $50,000 investment? In fact, here is another equation which covers this ground and sheds light on another technical term:

PRE-MONEY VALUATION
+ INVESTMENT AMOUNT
POST-MONEY VALUATION

Get it? The "post-money valuation" is merely the prior value of the startup plus the new money just invested.

But that doesn't tell us how to get out of the starting gate. How do we determine the "pre-money valuation"?

For companies which are sometimes called "going concerns" or "Main Street companies"—that is, established businesses which not only have revenues but also have profits—there are a variety of tried-and-true methods. Discounted cash flow, multiples of revenue, multiples of EBIDTA, and so on. Not necessarily the end point, but these are well-accepted methodologies which at least create a baseline for negotiation.

For the tech or life science startup, throw those out the window. They just don't apply.

So, what to do? Here's my advice: take a top-down rather than a bottom-up approach.

Say what?

14

Valuation (Setting the Table)

When you take a bottom-up approach, you focus on the current state of the startup and how it measures against the rest of the world. The founder points to the state of the product, the state of the tech, the state of the customers, the state of the team, and so on.

And of course that's the problem. All those things are half-baked—at best. So the founder is trying to show the investor a half-cooked chicken and half-boiled rice and half-stirred brownies—while suggesting that it's a delicious (and valuable) meal. The pitch is so easy to attack and disassemble that it's almost comical. By the time the investor is through, even if its pushback is soft and gentle, the founder will emerge frustrated, shaken, and demoralized.

What might the investor say? Something like, "Ok, so what you're telling me is what we have here is an incomplete management team with some key talent gaps and some key holes. A product which is still rickety, and a long ways from being feature rich and highly functional. Yeah, ok, maybe a couple of 'customers,' but you knew those folks already, so they aren't true third-party points of validation." And so on.

You can hear it, right? Maybe you've already heard it. It's just such an easy story to punch holes in.

So what to do?

Let's go top-down.

What's that?

That's pitching the dream.

That narrative usually goes something like this:

"Ok, Investor. Psyched to partner with you. So here's the deal. You said you want a 10X return? That means I need to turn your $50,000 into $500,000. Here's how I am going to do that.

Look at my total addressable market—my TAM—the specific part of the market where my customers live. Look who they are, how many there are, and what they are willing to spend on something like my product. Of course the science is inexact, and we are still learning, but we feel really good about these basic parameters.

And if you look at other companies that have built companies with a similar TAM and a similar go-to-market strategy, they have sold for anywhere from $60,000,000 to $600,000,000.

I think we can grow into that kind of big, massive company, too. I really do. But let's not build our baseline off that. Let's use the smaller $60,000,000 figure.

If we assume that $60,000,000 is what we sell our assets for (the gross proceeds), and if we assume liabilities of $10,000,000 (which is really high!), that leaves us with $50,000,000 in net proceeds for distribution to the owners.

If you want a check for $500,000, and there is $50,000,000 to distribute, that means you need to own 1% of the company at exit.

Building in some buffer for dilution (more on this below), let's say we sell you 4% right now. So that 4% today puts you in a position to own 1% at exit, and pull in the 10X you are looking for—and hopefully we do even better!"

Sound plausible? Good! Keep reading.

15

Actually Selling Shares

Here is what you have done. Back to the most recent formula laid out above:

$$\begin{array}{l} \text{PRE-MONEY VALUATION} \\ + \text{ INVESTMENT AMOUNT} \\ \hline \text{POST-MONEY VALUATION} \end{array}$$

If \$50,000 buys 4%, that means it represents 4% of the post-money valuation. Which means the post-money valuation is \$1,250,000.

Huh?

It's simple! See:

$$\$50{,}000 \,/\, \$1{,}250{,}000 = 4\%$$

And so, working backwards, that means the pre-money valuation is \$1,200,000. Looks like this:

$$\begin{array}{r} \$1{,}200{,}000 \\ + \quad \$50{,}000 \\ \hline \$1{,}250{,}000 \end{array}$$

Or flipped:

POST-MONEY VALUATION	\$1,250,000
- INVESTMENT AMOUNT	\$50,000
PRE-MONEY VALUATION	\$1,200,000

Now let's go back to our earlier formulas and finish the job:

$$\frac{\text{PRE-MONEY VALUATION}}{\text{PRE-MONEY TOTAL SHARES}} = \text{PRICE PER SHARE (PPS)}$$

$$\frac{\text{INVESTMENT AMOUNT}}{\text{PPS}} = \text{\# OF SHARES SOLD}$$

Populating the formulas:

$$\frac{\$1{,}200{,}000}{10{,}000{,}000} = \$0.12$$

$$\frac{\$50{,}000}{\$0.12} = 416{,}667$$

Boom!

So now what does our cap table look like? Here we go, all rolled up:

	COMMON	PREFERRED	TOTAL	%
A	6M	–	6M	57.60%
B	3M	–	3M	28.80%
C	1M	–	1M	9.60%
ANGEL	–	416,667	416,667	4.00%
	10M	416,667	10,416,667	100.00%

There is a lot here to unpack. We'll take it in pieces.

But first things first—nice job! First investor closed, and sold a pre-money valuation of $1,200,000. That means that, in theory, what existed before the deal, before the $50,000 investment, was equal to $1,200,000.

Was it REALLY worth that, based on what's literally in the asset basket RIGHT NOW? Honestly?

Probably not.

But what was sold was the dream. And when discounting back from the dream, we got to a present value of $1,200,000. Who said selling was hard?

What else do we see? We see three columns for shares. Common shares, preferred shares, and then total shares. The cool kids say that preferred shares convert into common shares "on a one-to-one basis." It just means they are the same when calculating ownership percentages. So we roll them all up into a single column. I call it total shares. If you really want to impress your friends, you can label that column "common share equivalents," or CSE for short.

More? Well, notice that the ownership percentages of the founders all dropped. Founder A went from owning 60% of the company to 57.60% of the company. Note that her share ownership was UNCHANGED. She started with 6,000,000 shares, and ended with 6,000,000 shares. That's confusing for some people. It's as simple as this—when the company sells shares, as it did here, it creates new shares. It doesn't pull shares from the existing owners.

Ok, fine. So the share numbers hold, but the ownership percentages dropped. That's called *dilution*. And that's what we were referencing in the conversation with the investor. The startup sold that investor 4% today on the assumption that between now and exit, the company will sell still more shares to raise still more money—which will dilute this investor too. So that 4% will drop a bit each time (just like that 60% dropped to 57.60%).

Anything else? Well, the numbers got ugly. We went from nice round easy numbers to rounding and decimals and some inelegance. I could have manipulated the example in this book to make it cleaner, but I didn't—because this is reality. This happens so quickly in a startup's life. The cap table gets, well, a little messy. Best to just get used to it.

Whew. That was a lot. Does it always unfold like this?

No.

What? Then why spill all this ink?

16

The Bottleneck

What if the parties can't get there on valuation—whether directly, or indirectly via ownership percentage as we illustrated above?

Well, that happens—it actually happens a lot. And you know when it really happened? The dotcom bubble.

Gen X remembers this well, Millennials a bit. Gen Z? Well, it may feel a little dinosaurish.

There once was a time, many many years ago (before 1996), when the internet was merely a message board for geeks. Then something called e-commerce started to emerge. That's right, if humans are good at anything, it's taking any kind of system or technology and figuring out how to use it to sell dog food.

So overnight, the startup popcorn popper went into overdrive. And these companies—informally called "dotcoms"—covered the earth.

Keep in mind that no one had yet figured out how to make money actually doing this thing. So if you have a whole bunch of dotcoms suddenly emerging, all with big plans and big ideas but no demonstrable or dependable way to generate revenue—well, the money to grow has got to come from somewhere. And that somewhere is the place from which it's always come—namely, investors.

Ok, so what's so different about this? Sounds pretty par for the course in Startupland.

The big difference was this—the absolute vacuum of information and history around business models, product development, product distribution, pricing, TAM—well, everything—meant that calculating valuation was virtually impossible.

Should the $50,000 investor receive 4% of the company as above? Or should it be 40%? Or 0.4%? Or something else?

No one knew.

Founders, buying in to the hype that this brand-new frontier promised billions to all, were out slinging visions of massive TAMs and massive exits. Which meant, of course, that they believed investor ownership percentages should be low. Translated: they were pitching very high pre-money valuations.

Investors were not immune. That's how bubbles become bubbles, which is what this dotcom thing developed into. And some jumped in feet first, buying in at whatever valuation the founders wanted.

But that wasn't true for most investors, particularly those with some level of sophistication and experience. They didn't want to miss out—they definitely had FOMO before FOMO was FOMO (FOMO-pre-FOMO?)—but they weren't willing to invest at just any price. They pushed back, albeit gently, because, hey, who wouldn't want the opportunity to invest in the first startup to sell shingles and roofing nails over the internet?

Ok, so what's the punchline? Well, it's as simple as this—no agreement on valuation, no way to sell shares. No way to sell shares, no way to take in the investor's cash. No way to take in the investor's cash, no way to build the company.

A bottleneck.

17

The Way Through

Yikes. Sounds bad. And it was.

Founders and investors alike called their attorneys (some may have emailed, but that kind of messaging was still reserved for the truly radical).

"Hey, so. Got this startup. Want to do this deal. Can't agree on valuation. What can we do?"

And attorneys do what they do best—they just said no.

"Yeah, wow. That's a tough one. Just go figure out the valuation. You gotta. No valuation, no way to do the deal."

"But we can't."

"Yeah, wow. Well, I see you are calling me using your long-distance calling card and that's pretty expensive (note: that was a thing), and I'm pretty expensive too, so, well, you go figure this out, and call me back when you have. I'm happy to do what I do best, which is mechanically push paper."

Rinse and repeat across the country.

But eventually the bottleneck was broken by the rarest of breeds, a breed which sometimes magically emerges in a wonderful accident of

Darwinian evolution. A creative lawyer stepped forth. And this person thought, "You know, our balance sheet looks like this:

Equity is off-limits because we can't agree on valuation. No valuation, no shares.

But there is another slot on that side of the balance sheet—liabilities.

How about instead of shares, we sell debt? In other words, our investors become lenders, and our startups become borrowers?"

Brilliant.

And thus was born the seed note.

18

The Seed Note

These instruments go by many names. Seed notes. Promissory notes. Or if the lawyer wants to sound unnecessarily fancy, debentures or bonds. But they all mean the same thing. It's debt. As simple as that.

The amount of the investment is called principal. In our example above, it would be $50,000.

The IRS insists that debt have both an interest rate and a maturity date. So you need those as well.

The interest rate could be lower than 5%, or higher than 20%, but in the vast majority of deals, it's 8% (maybe toggling as low as 6% or as high as 10%). And it has nothing to do with the current prime rate or the Fed or anything like that. It's just custom. Someone dropped 8% into a document 20 years ago, and it stuck. Why? This should sound familiar. That's right. Cumulative dividends. Similar concepts. Same numerical plugs.

The maturity date refers to the date on which the debt is due. This debt is not like a mortgage, or a car note. The borrower doesn't pay principal and interest on some kind of installment or amortized basis. It's all due at the end, at once. Some people call it a "balloon payment." Pop.

Culture rules here as well. No deep rationale, but the typical term is set to be 18–24 months. In THEORY, that date is supposed to align with the ultimate exhaustion of the capital raised, as well as the accomplishment of some business objective which positively tees up the next financing.

In REALITY, of course . . . well, you know . . . the best laid plans . . . (and more on the consequences, below).

So if it's 24 months, with 8% interest, and a principal amount of $50,000—then on the maturity date, the total amount owed by the borrower (the startup) to the lender (the investor) is $58,000. Principal plus 2 years' interest @ $4,000/year (I'm assuming simple interest; if it compounds, the total would be a nudge higher).

And that's it! Which was one of the unexpected but sticky benefits of the seed note—it's simple. Unlike preferred shares, which require a fair level of negotiation and paper (remember participating versus non-participating? protective provisions?), these seed notes are easy-peasy. Fewer terms to negotiate means fewer points of friction between the parties—and fewer items for lawyers to wrestle with. Quicker deals, cheaper deals.

That said, while everyone enjoyed an initial sense of euphoria, the feeling wore off quickly. Pretty soon, in fact, everyone was angry.

19

What Went Wrong with Seed Notes?

What was the problem?

Well, on the one hand, founders quickly found themselves in a pickle. Had they raised the money? Yes. Had they figured out a way to get it into the company, notwithstanding the stand-off on valuation? Yes. But . . .

That repayment obligation. Yikes.

Remember the introduction to this book (all those many pages ago!). These sorts of tech and life science startups raise money to invest it in R&D, product development, marketing, whatever—all with an eye on building long-term value that will be realized in an exit transaction, a liquidity event.

But they don't (typically) generate profits or free cash flow, especially in the short-term. In other words, no way will they be in a position to pay this seed note back at maturity. So the founders were terrified.

But at least the investors were happy, right? Wrong.

Investors like this don't invest in startups like this for 8% per year. Way too much risk for way too little upside. They want to be on the cap table—they want shares which represent their ownership percentage, which then map to their allocation of net proceeds at exit. The payoff promised here was just too little. So they were irritated.

So the founders and investors alike went back to the lawyers, looking for answers. And lawyers, once again, did what they do best—they just said no.

"Yeah, wow. That's a tough one. I get the terror/irritation. But it's debt. It is what it is."

"But it just replaces our first problem with a new problem."

"Yeah, wow. Well, I see you are calling me using your long-distance calling card and that's pretty expensive, and I'm pretty expensive too, so, well, you go figure this out, and call me back when you have. I'm happy to do what I do best, which is mechanically push paper."

But once again, the bottleneck was broken by a creative lawyer. And this person thought, "You know, our balance sheet looks like this:

And the parties ended up in "L," rather than "E," because they couldn't agree on valuation.

But what if we figured out a way to move the seed notes from "L" to "E." If we can turn the debt into shares, then the startup has no repayment obligation, and the investor gets that cap table upside."

And so the CONVERTIBLE seed note was born.

20

The Convertible Seed Note

These instruments go by many names. Convertible seed notes. Convertible promissory notes. Or, once again, if the lawyer wants to sound unnecessarily fancy, convertible debentures or convertible bonds. But they all mean the same thing. It's convertible debt. As simple as that.

Skeletally, you start with a basic seed note as described in Chapter 18. But then you jazz it up a bit. How?

You'll include a provision which says something like this: "If a Qualified Financing closes before the maturity date, then this convertible seed note will automatically convert into same preferred shares sold in that Qualified Financing, at the same price per share."

What's that "Qualified Financing" thing?

Any time you see a capitalized term in a legal document, it means it's defined somewhere. It means something very special. And locating and understanding that definition is important.

The convertible seed note will include a definition of "Qualified Financing." In spirit, a Qualified Financing is supposed to be an equity financing (that means a sale of shares, and in particular, preferred shares) which is sizable enough to suggest that the parties involved probably negotiated valuation at arms-length. In other words, it wasn't a $10 investment by Aunt Edna which fixed the valuation at $1 billion.

Amounts vary note to note and deal to deal, but Qualified Financings typically range from $250,000 to $2,500,000. Remember what we said above about the maturity date? That the date tends to tie to a certain anticipated inflection point? In THEORY, the Qualified Financing is supposed to represent the capital needed to push the company through and beyond that inflection point, to the next marker down the road. In REALITY, of course . . . well, you know . . . the best laid plans . . .

If you have yet to hear the phrase "it always costs twice as much and takes twice as long"—well, not only are you going to hear it (a lot), but you'll be living it. Maturity dates are routinely blown through, and Qualified Financings are routinely insufficient. But I digress . . .

Back to Qualified Financings. Ok, so it's a fixed amount of capital. What else? Well, it also comes later in time. It's raised after this convertible seed note, but before the maturity date. In other words, at a point in time when the negotiation of valuation is easier, simply because the company is a bit more mature and not so raw.

Ok, so that's the definition of Qualified Financing. Anything else we need to know? Yes, two other things.

First, go to the end of the provision where it says the conversion will take place "at the same price per share." That means that the seed note will convert into equity at the same price per share as the new money invested in the company.

So let's go back to our handy-dandy equations:

$$\frac{\text{PRE-MONEY VALUATION}}{\text{PRE-MONEY TOTAL SHARES}} = \text{PRICE PER SHARE (PPS)}$$

$$\frac{\text{INVESTMENT AMOUNT}}{\text{PPS}} = \text{\# OF SHARES SOLD}$$

Let's go back to our original example where our three founders issued themselves a total of 10,000,000 shares. And let's say for these purposes that the "Qualified Financing" was defined in the convertible seed note as $500,000, and it was later invested by one investor.

And that investor negotiated a pre-money valuation of $5,000,000 with the founders.

Ok. Take a breath. Recovered? Let's do this thing.

Our price per share is:

$$\frac{\$5{,}000{,}000}{10{,}000{,}000} = \$0.50$$

So the number of shares (specifically, preferred shares) sold to that investor in the Qualified Financing is:

$$\frac{\$500{,}000}{\$0.50} = 1{,}000{,}000$$

Got it: 1,000,000 preferred shares sold.

What's this mean for our convertible seed note?

Well, let's use our prior example. Let's say it's $50,000 in principal, and let's say it has accrued $5,000 in interest. If it converts in the Qualified Financing "at the same price per share," that means $0.50.

So:

$$\frac{\$55{,}000}{\$0.50} = 110{,}000$$

Our "investment amount" is principal plus interest (sometimes interest is repaid in cash and just the principal converts, but that's unusual). So our seed investor is issued 110,000 preferred shares.

See! You did it!

This stuff isn't that hard. Even when it's called a convertible bond.

Ok, I promised two other things. We just did one. What's the other?

The convertible seed note provision says that the note will "automatically" convert. That's important. It means that it "just happens." Specifically, it means that it happens without negotiation. That's a big deal, and important for founders. The fewer the points of negotiation, the better. If you have to negotiate for something, it means you want something. Which usually means you have to give something.

No negotiation? Then no give. Settled.

But this does raise an important final point—in our example, a Qualified Financing was set at $500,000. What if the total amount raised was only, say, $400,000?

By definition, that would not be a Qualified Financing. Sometimes a financing like that is creatively defined as a "Non Qualified Financing" (gee, thanks, lawyers). But that little difference means a lot.

In a non (or Non) Qualified Financing, the convertible seed note doesn't automatically convert. So if the new investors insist that the convertible seed note convert, then the founder has got to NEGOTIATE with the holder of that note.

Almost always, the new investors will indeed insist on this conversion. Why? Well, remember the balance sheet:

The new investors are purchasing shares. That puts them in the "E" quadrant. But if the convertible seed notes remain outstanding as notes, then they'll remain outstanding as debt—which means they'll sit in the "L" quadrant.

That means the old money (the convertible seed notes) will be "senior" to the new money (the preferred shares). Meaning they go first in the waterfall (remember that concept?). New investors hate that. As a general matter, new money wants to be senior to all other investor money—or at the very least, at the same level (we call that "pari passu" in the biz). It will not want to be junior.

So the founder will need to persuade the convertible seed note holder to voluntarily convert its convertible seed note into preferred shares—as if it were a Qualified Financing. More often than not, this is an easy conversation. The convertible seed note holder is happy to see the startup get funding and happy to play its part. But sometimes there is friction, and sometimes threading this needle is problematic. Sometimes it requires a give . . .

For this reason, founders want Qualified Financing thresholds to be *low*, and convertible seed note holders want them *high*. The lower the threshold, the more likely it is that the equity financing on deck will satisfy the criterion—which means that the convertible seed note conversion happens automatically.

Convertible seed note holders, on the other hand, don't mind the idea of having some say—because say means leverage. A higher threshold makes it more likely that an equity financing won't meet the Qualified Financing criterion—and so their consent, their permission, will be necessary. We all like to be in control, eh?

DILUTION AND PRO RATA RIGHTS

We have already covered the concept of "dilution" within the context of the sale of new shares. If you own 6,000,000 common shares, and there are a total of 10,000,000 shares issued and outstanding, then you own 60% of the company. If the company then sells an additional 2,000,000 preferred shares, you still own your 6,000,000 common shares, but the total shares increase from 10,000,000 to 12,000,000—and so your ownership percentage drops from 60% to 50%. That's dilution.

No one likes dilution. But it's a fact of startup life. That said, investors have developed two means by which they try to at least diminish its impact on themselves.

The hard one first: "anti-dilution protection." A deceptively simple label. Take a breath, then read on.

You'll sometimes see this concept embedded in preferred shares at the seed deal level. You will ALWAYS see it in "Series A" Preferred Shares and beyond. Remember the earlier sidebar on Venture Capital Preferred Stock Financings and the NVCA? You'll find this term in the Certificate of Incorporation.

Put simply, this provision will adjust the sacrosanct 1:1 formula between common shares and preferred shares that we discussed earlier in the book. It will "bump up" the relative value of a preferred share, so that it "converts" into MORE than one common share, but ONLY in the event of what is called a "down round."

What's that? A down round is an informal way of describing a later financing where shares are sold at a price lower than the price originally paid by the existing preferred shareholders.

If it's "full ratchet anti-dilution protection," then those existing preferred shareholders are fully insulated from the impact of the down round. So if they originally paid $1.00 per share, and if the down round priced at $0.50 per share, then instead of converting into one common share, each preferred share will now convert into two common shares. Full ratchets are rare (which is good, because the name alone sounds like something from a Salem witch trial).

The more typical approach is . . . wait for it . . . "weighted average anti-dilution protection." Great branding . . .

The math is beyond this book's scope, but the basic idea is that the conversion formula adjusts based on the depth of the down round and the size of the financing. If it's a massive financing at $0.50 per share, then the adjustment may indeed push the conversion formula awfully close to 1:2 (as with a full ratchet). But if the discount is relatively small and/or the financing relatively small, it may be more like 1:1.1 or 1.2, or something like that. The idea is to give the existing preferred shareholders SOME accommodation, but not COMPLETE protection.

Ok, whew. That was the hard one. What's the easy one?

These are called "pro rata rights," "participation rights," "preemptive rights," or, sometimes, "rights of first refusal." The basic idea is to give existing preferred shareholders the opportunity—the right—to participate in any future financing. To what extent? To the extent necessary for them to maintain their ownership percentage.

So if they own 10% of the company before the financing, then they would have the opportunity to participate in that financing and to buy that number of new shares necessary to keep them at 10%. That way they don't suffer dilution like, say, the founder did above, in going from 60% to 50%.

What's crucial to understand is that this is *not* a free ride. These existing preferred shareholders must pay for these shares—and there is no bargain. They pay what the new investors pay. They simply have the right to participate. And if they do, while it'll cost them, they will protect themselves from dilution.

Do founders ever get pro rata rights? They can. If they ask for those rights, they are rarely turned down. And even without those rights, if they ask to participate in a later financing, they are rarely turned down. Investors tend to like to see founders invest money in their own companies. They see it as a good thing, a vote of confidence.

That being said, both the right itself and participation itself are very rare among founders. Why? Because, well, founders are, shall we say, "resource constrained." Right. They are poor. They tend not to have the nickels necessary to make these investments. And that's ok!

21

Is That It?

So now we understand the origin story of convertible seed notes.

It all started with an inability to reach agreement on valuation, which meant the startup couldn't sell shares. But it could sell debt—a seed note. But founders and investors alike didn't like the simple seed note because it had to be repaid in cash (terror for the founders) and because the only upside was basic interest (irritation for the investors). So the CONVERTIBLE seed note was born.

In this original iteration of the convertible seed note, principal and interest automatically convert into the same preferred shares sold in a Qualified Financing, at the same price per share. If instead it's a non (or Non) Qualified Financing, then the same conversion formula holds, except that the permission of the convertible seed note holder is required.

Easy. So it's a wrap, right? Why are there more pages left in this book?

Well, remember the investor irritation around simple seed notes? We solved that original irritation by figuring out how to get those notes converted into shares so those investors could indeed participate in the upside. But a new irritation soon emerged.

(There's always something . . .)

22

Discounts

What quickly began to trouble investors is the sense that they were being played for fools. In this case, why should they buy shares at the same price as the new investors in the Qualified Financing?

Intuitively, they were sensing something like this:

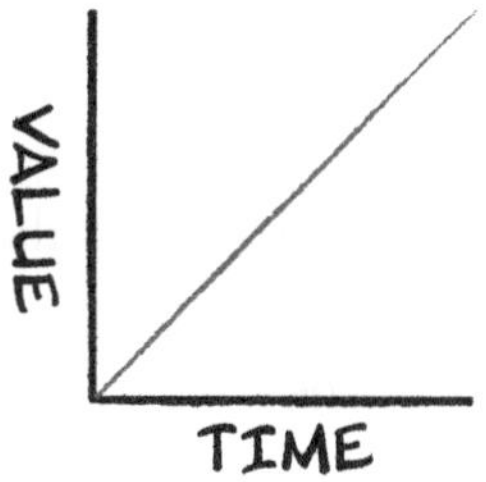

What are we looking at here?

The basic idea is that the value of the startup grows over time. It would be wonderful if it were always this steady—and always sloped this way! That's indeed the hope. And sometimes it works out like this, but sometimes it looks more like an EKG. And sometimes it's inverted (not good . . .).

Ok, fine. What's the point?

Because the value of the company grows over time, so too does the share price. We know this because we know the role valuation plays in the determination of price per share.

So what does this have to do with investor irritation? It's simply this:

The new money shows up later in time and sets a valuation which is higher than the valuation of the startup at the time the convertible seed note holder originally invested. Even though the convertible seed note holder and the startup couldn't agree on that valuation—hence the convertible seed note—intuitively it's pretty obvious that the valuation was lower. How much lower, who knows. But lower. Which means the convertible seed note holder is "paying" too high a price now, at the moment of conversion.

And that came to irritate convertible seed note holders. They felt like suckers.

And no one likes to feel like a sucker.

So no matter the swag the startup gave them (branded t-shirts!), or the love and gratitude, these convertible seed note holders were irritated. Highly irritated. And were determined not to repeat this practice in the next generation of convertible seed notes.

What was the answer?

The discount.

It's a brute force solution, but it does get at the issue.

Let's revisit our example above. The new money investor negotiated a pre-money valuation of $5,000,000 with the founders.

So our price per share is:

$$\frac{\$5{,}000{,}000}{10{,}000{,}000} = \$0.50$$

So the number of shares (specifically, preferred shares) sold to that investor is:

$$\frac{\$500{,}000}{\$0.50} = 1{,}000{,}000$$

Got it? 1,000,000 preferred shares.

What's this mean for our convertible seed note?

Assume it's $50,000 in principal and has accrued $5,000 in interest. If it converts in the Qualified Financing "at the same price per share," that means $0.50.

So:

$$\frac{\$55{,}000}{\$0.50} = 110{,}000$$

So our convertible seed note holder is issued 110,000 preferred shares.

But if there is a discount, the convertible seed note does NOT convert "at the same price per share." It converts at a discounted price.

The discount can be whatever the parties want it to be. It can be 5%, or it can be 50%, or whatever. But in most deals, the discount is 20%.

Any magic to that? No.

Science? No.

Someone dropped it in a document a generation ago, and it's held.

What comes next is technical, but important. If our discount here is 20%, then the convertible seed note will convert "at the same price per share discounted by 20%," or put differently, "at the same price per share multiplied by 0.80." It gets you to the same result, but it's important to read with care.

Why?

Well, let's work through our example. Instead of $0.50, the converting price per share (incorporating the 20% discount) will be $0.40. So:

$$\frac{\$55{,}000}{\$0.40} = 137{,}500$$

137,500 shares is more than 110,000—so you can see why the convertible seed note holder likes the idea of a discount!

But what if the drafters of the convertible seed note were not careful. What if they intended a 20% discount and wrote "at the same price per share multiplied by 0.20"?

Well, then the converting price per share won't be $0.40. It'll be $0.10! And the convertible seed note holder won't get 137,500 shares—they will get 550,000 shares! They will REALLY be happy. They'll be ecstatic. But the founders won't be—and it's not the deal.

The point: be careful. Discounts are either presented as a percentage reduction, or as a fractional multiplier. Make sure you determine how the math is done—and what factor you are inserting. A mistake here can cost you dearly!

So we are done then, right? Seems like everyone is happy?

Well, let me ask you this question. You know how you really wanted to buy that one thing last year? And you were super excited when you got it? You always noticed it, made sure it was clean, gazed at it lovingly? Do you still?

Nope.

It's called hedonic assimilation, and it's the plague of modern humanity. We want something, we get it—we are happy for a moment—and then we "assimilate" it. It becomes part of our baseline. It no longer makes us happy. It's effectiveness is neutered. So we need a new thing. We crave something more. And so on.

Happened here as well. Darn human nature!

23

Caps

So time marches on. We started with simple seed notes. Then moved to convertible seed notes. Then moved to convertible seed notes with a discount.

Note (heh) that this evolution is not marked by days or weeks—or even months. It's years. So what began in the midst of the late 90s dotcom bubble reached its final form in the aftermath of the Great Recession, when the world—and valuations—began to recover.

Remember our graph?

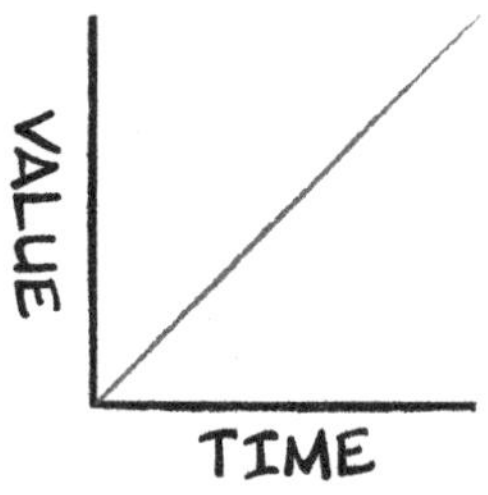

When times are rough and valuations flatten, early investors aren't as pressed by the "overpaying" scenario we charted above. The discount is enough—sometimes even more than enough—to satisfy everyone. But when that pitch steepens, when valuations start coursing upward at a more rapid rate, well, our friendly neighborhood convertible seed note holders start to get antsy.

And that's what happened circa 2010–2011. Bottom line, these folks no longer believed that the discount was enough. Yes, it was helpful. Yes, 137,500 shares is better than 110,000. But still . . .

You see, they had "assimilated" this goodness. They needed something more.

So what these convertible seed note holders said is, "Look, under no circumstances will our convertible seed notes convert at a valuation above a certain level. Even with a discount, we are still routinely above that valuation marker, which means we are paying too much. We need a limit. We need a ceiling. We need a CAP."

Caps are expressed as valuations. So the language of our convertible seed note gets a little more complicated. It will read something like this: the convertible seed note will convert "at the lesser of (1) the same price per share discounted by X%, or (2) a price per share calculated on the basis of a pre-money valuation of $Z."

Never easy, eh? Ok, let's shine some light on this by getting back to our equations and back to our example. I think by now you'll be able to track this easily. Starting to really sink in, right?

$$\frac{\text{PRE-MONEY VALUATION}}{\text{PRE-MONEY TOTAL SHARES}} = \text{PRICE PER SHARE (PPS)}$$

$$\frac{\text{INVESTMENT AMOUNT}}{\text{PPS}} = \text{\# OF SHARES SOLD}$$

$$\frac{\$5{,}000{,}000}{10{,}000{,}000} = \$0.50$$

$$\frac{\$500{,}000}{\$0.50} = 1{,}000{,}000$$

So what's happening here? The new money in the Qualified Financing is investing $500,000 on a $5,000,000 pre-money valuation. And the number of shares outstanding before this transaction is 10,000,000. All of which work out to a price per share of $0.50 for the new investors, and consequently the sale to the new investors of 1,000,000 new preferred shares.

You got this!

Now let's say that the convertible seed note has $55,000 of converting principal and interest, and it says this: the convertible seed note will convert "at the lesser of (1) the same price per share discounted by 20%, or (2) a price per share calculated on the basis of a pre-money valuation of $2,000,000."

Well, let's peel it apart. We have already calculated part one above. a price per share of $0.40 (20% off $0.50) results in the issuance to the convertible seed note holder of 137,500 new preferred shares.

How's the cap work in part two? Easy. We go back to our base formula, and instead of using $5,000,000 as the pre-money valuation, we substitute the $2,000,000. Looks like this:

$$\frac{\text{PRE-MONEY VALUATION}}{\text{PRE-MONEY TOTAL SHARES}} = \text{PRICE PER SHARE (PPS)}$$

$$\frac{\text{INVESTMENT AMOUNT}}{\text{PPS}} = \text{\# OF SHARES SOLD}$$

$$\frac{\$2{,}000{,}000}{10{,}000{,}000} = \$0.20$$

$$\frac{\$55{,}000}{\$0.20} = 275{,}000$$

So with the discount, the convertible seed note holder would get the benefit of a $0.40 price per share. But with the cap, the convertible seed note holder would get the benefit of a price per share of $0.20. They get the lesser, and so the latter.

Why? Because they want the lesser! Because the use of the lesser gives them 275,000 shares rather than 137,500 shares. That's a big swing!

The bigger the pre-money valuation for the new money, the more likely it is that the convertible seed note holder does better with the cap than with the discount. Why? Because the discount won't be enough to reduce the conversion price to the level at which the cap sits.

The discount really only comes into play if the pre-money valuation is awfully close to the cap. In that case, the discount works to take the convertible seed note's converting price per share below the price produced by the cap, and so that would be the winner there.

Whew. A lot of words, a lot of jargon, a lot of math. But that's it! You did it! You now know the key pivot points within every convertible seed note negotiation—and not only that, you understand where they came from, and why. But that last point leaves us with a hanging question, does it not?

For those of you not interrupted by drink service or by a talkative captain on your flight, who have been able to follow this portion of the book straight-through without interruption—you have likely identified a weird anomaly:

Simple seed notes, and then convertible seed notes, were introduced because founders and early investors could not agree on valuation. And these instruments solved that problem—first simply by being made convertible, and then through the inclusion of a discount. But this cap thing is expressed as valuation, and even gets inserted into the formula in lieu of the new money's pre-money valuation. So if it's a substitute for valuation, doesn't that make it a sorta-kinda valuation? And if that's the case—well, haven't we come full circle? Are we not negotiating valuation?

Yes! Yes we are!

24

• • •

Then Why Notes?

We are indeed negotiating valuation.

Now, we could spill ink drawing distinctions between caps and valuations. Folks will say that caps aren't really *present* valuations, that they are aspirational, that they are generic and not specific to this startup, that they are a convenient mathematical placeholder but not really valuations per se. And so on.

And those folks would not necessarily be wrong.

But it really doesn't matter. Because substantively, caps are valuations. They get swapped into our equations in the same place. That's how they are used, and that's how they function. And here, because we are talking dollars and cents and not theoretical physics, use and function equals reality.

"But how can that be?" you might say. Convertible seed notes were literally created to cover the inability of the parties to negotiate and agree on valuation. But now they include a term which requires the negotiation and agreement on valuation? Does that not knock the legs out from underneath the whole edifice?

Great question! I'm glad you asked.

Bottom line, the emergence of caps would indeed fatally undermine the convertible seed note if the original rationale were still the ongoing rationale.

Huh?

Recall the dotcom context. There was an absolute vacuum of information and history around business models, product development, product distribution, pricing, TAM—in other words, everything. Which meant that calculating valuation was virtually impossible.

But by the time of the introduction of the cap in 2010–2011, this was no longer the case. The venture industry had almost 15 years—across two bull markets and two recessions—to get some experience. That experience meant data, and that data meant that valuations could indeed be determined.

Well, great! So the bottleneck was resolved, and shares could be sold. Yippee!

Which is true. And we certainly have seen, in the years since, many more of these deals done as sales of preferred shares than we did in the preceding era.

But that being said: convertible seed notes not only remain as an alternative, but more often than not, seed deals are still done this way rather than via the sale of preferred shares.

Well that seems kinda weird.

And it is, kinda, until you consider the context. These seed deals tend not to involve a lot of money. The great thing about a convertible seed note is that there is not much to negotiate. Interest rate and maturity date? Maybe a little, but those are pretty well fixed as we discussed above. Discounts? Same. The only real point of negotiation is the cap.

But that's the case in a preferred share deal as well, right? Yes, except there it will be called valuation. But on top of that you also have all the economic and governance rights which swirl around preferred shares. It's just a more complicated instrument. Not massively more complicated. But it could be the difference between paying lawyers $5,000 to get a convertible seed note deal done versus $10,000 (or more) for a preferred share deal. And if the amount to be invested is $50,000, well, that difference means a lot.

Hence the change in rationale.

Convertible seed notes are no longer strictly needed as a way to bridge a valuation gap. Instead, they are useful because, simply put, they are simpler than preferred shares. Which makes them cheaper.

Ok, got it. But why is this not the end of the story? I can see more pages in the book!

Because, my friends, if you have learned anything at this point, it's that financing structures evolve. They don't sit still. And that will continue to be the case. Preferred shares may be preferred shares, and convertible seed notes may have pretty well frozen into a stable instrument, but that doesn't mean that there aren't other new market entrants.

But wait, how can that be?

Convertible seed notes are debt. Preferred shares are equity. Those are the two—and only two—quadrants on the righthand side of the balance sheet. There's no room for anything else, right?

Wrong.

But first we need to shift gears into a topic which is highly relevant and critically important but only adjacent to the matter of financing structures. What's that, you may say?

Stock options.

Bear with me. This will take a few chapters, but it'll tee-up the final seed deal structure that we need to cover, and along the way, you'll also be educated in an important element of startup capitalization—namely, equity compensation. It's a twofer!

25

Equity Compensation

Ok, we have applied the brakes, and we are shifting gears. We aren't raising money or talking financing structures. But what we are going to talk about still involves the cap table. And it all ties back together. Trust me!

So what is this equity compensation stuff, and stock options, and all that jazz?

Remember way back at the beginning of this book when we created our initial cap table? And we issued 6,000,000 common shares (the "founder shares") to Founder A because she wanted to wear her 60% ownership interest baller-style, not as some impoverished dummy-with-only-6-common-shares?

Well, those shares have value. We hope in the future they will have a TON of value. But right now, even today, at the very beginning, they have value. They are worth something.

So one of two things will happen. Either Founder A will buy them from the company, or they will be issued directly to Founder A in exchange for services.

What, you say! A startup gouges its own founders?

No, not exactly. Because if you do things right and get this company organized and these shares teed-up early enough, the company has virtually no value. Like, maybe $100 total. Nothing has happened yet! So that 60% is worth $60.

Founder A can cut the company a check for that, or she can report that $60 as ordinary income and pay taxes on it. Let's use a rate of 33%. In that case, she'd pay the IRS $20 in taxes. So yeah, money is money, but it's not back-breaking.

Taxes? Did I say taxes? I did. And we are going to talk a bit more about this. Buckle up, buttercup.

26

Death and . . .

We have worked to avoid getting mired in really ugly legal stuff in this book ("Huh, doesn't feel that way to me," you are surely thinking . . .).

Section 83(a) of the Internal Revenue Code provides in part as follows (this is important for what comes later, so please read this excerpt and don't skip over it):

"If, in connection with the performance of services, property is transferred to any person . . ., the excess of (1) the fair market value of such property . . . over (2) the amount (if any) paid for such property, shall be included in the gross income of the person who performed such services . . ."

So if Founder A got the shares, and the fair market value is $60, but she paid $60, then there is nothing to include in income ($60 – $60 = $0). But if she paid $0, she would include $60 in income ($60 – $0 = $60).

No big deal, right?

Right!

But what happens as time marches on? Well, hopefully, the value of the company goes up!

So let's say we reach that moment where Founders A, B, and C want to add a fourth contributor. Let's call that person Employee 1. And everyone is excited! There's really something here now. The company is churning along and needs more arms and legs to grow and prosper. And the founders have found precisely the right person. This is something to celebrate!

And of course, as part of their package, Employee 1 wants equity, and the founders want her to have equity. Partly because Employee 1 is probably not being paid much in cash, but mainly because early employees like this are like founders and investors. They want upside! They want some of those net proceeds on exit!

This is what "equity compensation" means. In exchange for services, that person is paid in equity. Maybe not solely in equity (probably not), but equity is a meaningful part of her overall compensation package.

So getting back to our example. Let's say the conversations and negotiations are complete, and Employee 1 is going to get equity representing 10% of the startup.

Well, think waaaaaay back to our initial discussion of valuation. Remember this equation?

PRE-MONEY VALUATION
+ INVESTMENT AMOUNT

POST-MONEY VALUATION

Recall how sometimes we worked a bottom-up process? When a founder would say, "Hey, the seed investor wants to invest $200,000 for 10%"? And remember how we needed to walk that back to a pre-money valuation so that we could calculate how many preferred shares that seed investor was to be issued (because we want that cap table tight and right!).

That would mean the post-money valuation is $2,000,000 ($200,000 / $2,000,000 = 10%), which means the pre-money valuation is $1,800,000 ($2,000,000 – $200,000 = $1,800,000, from the bottom-up).

Any tax to be paid? Putting aside the question of services, the answer is no, regardless, because the investor paid $200,000 for something worth $200,000. The net difference was $0, so no tax.

So how does that relate here?

Employee 1 is getting 10% of the company, and, for precisely the same reasons (ownership percentages! allocation of net proceeds!), we need to determine how many shares represent 10%—in this case, common shares and not preferred shares—because the shares are being issued for services and not for money, but still. We need a number. So we need a valuation.

What am I saying? We need to determine what 10% is worth. If the company has a post-money valuation of $2,000,000 (or in this case, "post equity compensation valuation"), then that 10% must be worth $200,000.

If Employee 1 pays nothing for the shares, which is usually the case, because remember, it's equity compensation (and not an investment transaction), well . . .

According to Section 83(a) of the Internal Revenue Code, you take shares worth $200,000 and deduct from that the price paid (here, $0) . . . and so you end up needing to include $200,000 in the gross income of Employee 1.

If 33% is her rate, then she will need to pay the IRS $66,667 in taxes.

What?!?

27

Fear, Uncertainty, and Doubt

That $200,000 in shares is treated exactly the same as if she had been paid $200,000 in cash. The IRS doesn't distinguish cash from shares—or from cows or eggs, for that matter. The term in Section 83(a) is "property," and it's expansive and inclusive.

When the startup issued shares to the founders, they were issued common shares, and as we discussed, you'll sometimes hear people refer to them informally as "founder shares." Another term for them is "restricted shares." That's a term that applies to any shares awarded by the startup in exchange for services.

Not surprisingly, they are called "restricted" because there are certain "restrictions" placed upon those shares under the securities laws, mainly relating to limitations on the right to transfer or sell the shares. Not terribly relevant in the real world, and certainly not for purposes of this book, because we are all about the exit, so don't sweat it.

At a high level, the award of restricted shares is the best form of equity compensation because the recipient gets the shares immediately, and this starts her holding period under the tax laws (which is important because, generally speaking, the longer the recipient holds the shares, the lower the rate that will apply on the eventual sale of those shares).

But there is a catch. The issuance of restricted shares is only practical if the shares can be issued at a time when the value of the company is relatively low. Why? Because they won't cost much (if the recipient is paying for them directly), or the tax will be low (if the recipient is just being awarded them without payment).

This is how it works for founders, and this is why founder SHARES are the norm.

And it may be, even for the "post-founder" people added in the early days, that a low value is still defensible, and so those folks can get restricted shares. Yay!

But there will come a point when it's just not feasible. And for a good reason—because the startup is actually getting things done and creating value. Yay! But also, boo!

So what is to be done? Entrance: stock options.

CONTRIBUTION OF INTELLECTUAL PROPERTY

When founders organize their Delaware "C" corporations, they are faced with a handful of key documents.

Two are the Certificate of Incorporation and Bylaws. The former is the public document filed in Delaware, the filing of which literally creates the corporation. The latter is an internal document. Between the two, the basic matters of governance and economics are covered.

The founders will also sign some kind of agreement covering the issuance of their founder shares, including any terms, conditions, and restrictions on those founder shares.

Finally, they will sign some kind of agreement by which they agree to keep the company's confidential information, well, confidential. It may also include restrictive covenants like a promise not to solicit the company's employees or customers on behalf of a competitor—and perhaps a promise not to compete, period.

That agreement will also include a provision by which the founder agrees to assign to the company all intellectual property created or conceived by her. This is critically important.

First things first—intellectual property (often shortened to "IP") is a massive category. It's not simply patents, trademarks, and copyrights, although those are certainly important and well-known types of IP. It also reaches trade secrets, know-how, ideas, inventions, and so on. Think of it as anything intangible. If it's important to the business and isn't something that you can literally touch—there is a good chance it's IP.

The default rule in most places is that employers own the intellectual property created by their employees. But contractors, on the other hand, *personally* own the intellectual property they create! For tech and life science startups, intellectual property sits at the heart and soul of the company. There can be no ambiguity or risk around ownership. The company must own it, and own it all. Hence, regardless of position, station, or circumstances, every person in every role—whether employee or contractor—must be asked to sign an agreement like this.

Sometimes, the founders have been at the project which underlies the budding startup for some time before formal organization. Consequently, they may have collectively created something of value already.

If this is the case, then by signing the assignment of IP agreement, they are not only assigning future IP, but the founders are also assigning pre-existing IP. Sometimes, that IP can be characterized as the consideration paid for the founder shares.

For instance, it may be that the pre-existing IP is attributed a value of $1,000. If that's the case, then it can be used as currency by the founders to "buy" their founder shares.

I would not advise proceeding down such a path without careful consultation with a lawyer and, especially, an accountant. It can sometimes create valuation challenges of the sort we just discussed in the preceding chapters. But it's sometimes a viable and attractive strategy.

And regardless—attend to that IP. Make sure it all gets assigned to the company!

28

Stock Options

First things first. In startups, particularly startups which aspire to attract traditional venture capital, there are certain ways that things are done.

One of these is organizing as a Delaware "C" corporation. We made reference to this earlier in this book. It doesn't matter if you've done extensive research and deep analysis and determined that, for your purposes, a Massachusetts Business Trust is the perfect form. Nope.

There's method to the madness here. Sometimes for legal and technical reasons. Sometimes for reasons of scalability and market expectations. And sometimes just due to culture and custom. Trust me. Don't rock this boat. Stay in the groove.

Same with equity compensation. You may have heard of things like stock appreciation rights, phantom stock, employee stock ownership plans, restricted units, and so on. These are real things, and these and others are alternative methods of equity compensation.

But not for you!

In Startupland, we have two choices: restricted shares or stock options. That's it. Trust me. Don't rock this boat. Stay in the groove.

Ok, so with that said, what the heck are stock options?

An option is a right to buy stock. Sometimes it's called a "derivative security" (by people who want to sound fancy). It means its relevance and its value are tied to another security. Here, common shares.

There is another term for the right to buy stock that you may have heard—a warrant. It's the same thing as an option.

And just like common shares and preferred shares show up in the "equity" portion of the balance sheet, that's where options and warrants are recorded as well.

Ok, now what comes next is very high level. The tax issues can get a little hairy, and context and facts matter—which can impact the tax analysis. But still, generally speaking, here are the basics:

Every option and every warrant will include some basic terms. Remember our discussion of convertible seed notes? They all include principal amount, interest rate, and maturity date—along with, where applicable, discounts and caps. Similar thing here.

When the holder of an option actually purchases the shares to which the option is attached, that's called an "option exercise." It has nothing to do with free weights or cardio. All it means is that the holder says, "Hey, this option gives me the right to buy X number of shares. I want to buy them—so I want to EXERCISE my option." Sometimes these shares are called "option shares." So we need to know the number of option shares.

We also need to know the purchase price—or, not surprisingly, sometimes called the "exercise price," or even more vividly, the "strike price." When the holder wants to exercise the option, what's the purchase price per share? This is what we are getting at here.

We also need to know the term of the option. This is analogous to the maturity date of a convertible seed note. At some point, the option terminates, or expires. (We'll cut to the chase on this one. It can vary, but the term is typically 5–10 years.)

Finally, we need to know if the option "vests." I understand suits, you may be saying, but I thought vests were out of fashion. What the heck?

29

• • •

Vesting

So "vesting," in the context of stock options, has nothing to do with keeping your body core extra warm. Whew.

Here, "vesting" means that the right to exercise the option is conditional. It's conditioned on the accomplishment of something.

It can be based on performance. The option could say, for instance, that it vests and becomes exercisable in full when the recipient successfully sells 100 boxes of cookies. So long as the recipient accomplishes that objective at some point during the term of the option, she would then be permitted to exercise the option—in other words, actually purchase the underlying shares.

The recipient does not need to exercise right away. She can wait. But she cannot exercise BEFORE the condition is met.

Performance vesting is great because it aligns, with a high level of precision, key business objectives with the activities of the recipient. When the recipient accomplishes something which creates value, she gets value in exchange. Perfect calibration.

There are cases where an option allows for something called "early exercise," but that's a more technical and advanced concept, and not something we need to cover here. But just know it exists.

All that being said: most of the time, vesting is measured by, well, time.

In Startupland, a typical approach reads something like this: "This option vests over 4 years, with a one-year cliff and then monthly thereafter."

A cliff? Yikes!

It's not that bad. Let's unpack it. For these purposes, let's assume the number of option shares is 480.

On day 1, the recipient is vested into nothing. Day 32, nothing. Day 267, nothing. Day 363, nothing.

At the end of one year of service, however, the recipient vests into 25% of the option shares—here, 120 shares. That means she now has the right, at will, to purchase 120 option shares at the exercise price.

Then over the next three years, the remaining option shares will vest monthly—so that's the 360 option shares remaining divided by 36 months (so, 10 shares per month).

The cliff is there as a probationary period of sorts. If the recipient doesn't work out, then she won't have the chance to exercise her options or have any ownership in the company.

The four-year term is there to keep her around. If the recipient wants the chance to purchase all the option shares, then she must stick around for four years. That's what the company wants. They don't want to award this person options to purchase 480 shares on Monday, have her exercise the options and buy all the shares on Tuesday, and then quit on Wednesday. The company wants to keep her around, working hard. This vesting schedule creates an incentive for the recipient to stay onboard. That's why options are sometimes referred to as "incentive equity."

At 30,000 feet, there is a heavy bias for performance-vesting. Who cares about whether someone just shows up every day, right? What matters is what she actually accomplishes, and she should be rewarded for that.

True, but performance-vesting requires precision. If there is any ambiguity around the vesting criteria—or if the business pivots and the original criteria are no longer relevant—then these programs can be a disaster. Friction. Disputes. Potential litigation.

Bleck.

Hence, time-vesting. Yeah, not as tailored as performance-vesting, but it certainly is easy to measure. And unambiguous. With the basic notion being, look, if the person is performing, doing what she needs to do, then she will remain employed. So in a blunt and indirect sense, time-vesting is indeed a form of performance-vesting.

Remember how discounts in the context of convertible seed notes were a brute-force way to approximate an early valuation? Same idea here. Time-vesting is a brute-force way to approximate performance.

A few other tidbits about vesting:

- Once vested, an option must be exercised during its term. That is, if the option expires unexercised, it's gone.
- If awarded in connection with employment, options will usually include a requirement that they must be exercised, if at all, within a certain period after employment ends. The tax laws vary on what is required, and context and market matter as well, but the usual rule of thumb is that vested options must be exercised within three months of employment termination (note that unvested options simply expire at employment termination, period).
- "Acceleration" is a term you sometimes hear. It's usually tied to a liquidity event or exit transaction. Recall the entire foundation of this book: the equity portion of the balance sheet is where the owners live, and the shares held by the owners dictate their respective ownership percentages, which in turn drive the allocation of net proceeds on exit. The more shares you own, the higher your ownership percentage—so the more proceeds you get! But what if the option isn't fully vested when this moment happens? Out of luck?

  Well, sometimes options will include language which allows for acceleration, meaning the automatic vesting of some or all of the unvested shares, so that the holder can buy those option shares (and accordingly increase her ownership percentage). There are different ways this can be structured, different criteria that can be put in place, but this is the basic idea.
- Not all options vest. Sometimes options are awarded "fully vested." In the case of options which are issued as part of an investment transaction (more on this below), these are typi-

cally fully vested. But even in the case of options for services, sometimes circumstances call for them to be fully vested—or at least partially vested right out of the gate. And that's all perfectly acceptable.

- Restricted shares can vest!

Wait, what? I thought we were done with restricted shares?

Nope!

Gotcha.

30

Restricted Shares and Section 83(b)

We want to use options to incentivize performance. We don't just want to award a person options with an immediate right to exercise. Remember the hypo above: rarely would we want to award a person options to purchase, say, 480 shares on Monday, have her exercise the options and buy all the shares on Tuesday, and then quit on Wednesday.

You want to keep her around, working hard. The vesting schedule creates an incentive for the recipient to stay onboard.

That's why options are sometimes referred to as "incentive equity."

And that all holds true for restricted shares as well. Even founder shares.

Maybe even MORE SO for founder shares!

Say what?

Consider this. Our initial cap table. We had three founders: one with 60%, one with 30%, and the other with 10%.

What if that third founder left on day 2? Well, if there is no vesting, she will leave with a full 10% of the company.

Ouch.

Which means the other two founders will need to issue more shares to recruit a replacement—and because the total share number will increase, everyone's ownership percentage will drop. Ouch.

But even worse, frankly, those remaining founders will be working every day to create wealth for that MIA third founder. Want to meet a cranky founder? All you need to do is find a founder in this situation. It's grinding. It's painful. It feels incredibly unfair and inequitable.

There are various solutions, but the most elegant, and the most typical, is vesting. Simply make the restricted shares subject to vesting. That way, if a founder bails, she won't walk away with everything. Only with the shares into which she has vested.

But beware.

Remember Section 83(a) of the Internal Revenue Code? I've pasted below the portion we quoted above, with additional language included in gray that I did not include originally. Now it's time to wrestle with it:

"If, in connection with the performance of services, property is transferred to any person . . ., the excess of (1) the fair market value of such property . . . at the first time the rights of the person having the beneficial interest in such property . . . are not subject to a substantial risk of forfeiture . . . over (2) the amount (if any) paid for such property, shall be included in the gross income of the person who performed such services in the first taxable year in which the rights of the person having the beneficial interest in such property . . . are not subject to a substantial risk of forfeiture . . ."

Eyes . . . glazing . . . over . . .

Believe me, I get it. But this is super important.

Vesting represents a "substantial risk of forfeiture." So what Section 83(a) is saying is this: if the shares are subject to vesting, the recipient doesn't need to pay tax on them until the shares vest.

Seems awesome, right?

Well, yes, but only if the value of the shares remains flat, and we definitely don't want to assume that.

If you got fully vested shares, and the fair market value is $60, and you paid $0, you would include $60 in income. No big deal, right?

Right.

But let's say those shares are subject to four-year vesting with a one-year cliff. So there would be no tax at award. Yay!

But you would be taxed on the value of the 15 shares you vested into at the end of year one. Ok, cool—just $15 in taxable value, right?

Probably not.

Because the value is calculated at that moment, not as of the time of the original award. So if those 60 shares are now worth $10 per share, and rather than $1 per share, you'd pay tax on $150 of value, not $15.

Ok, not great, but still, not that big a deal, right?

Right—but what if this startup is the proverbial unicorn. The 60 shares are now worth $6,000,000. Yay!

But also, boo!!!

Why?

Because you, my friend, need to pay tax on $1,500,000 in value. At a 33% rate, that means you need to write the IRS a check for $500,000. This year. Now.

Whoa!!!

Exactly.

"How do I avoid this?" you might be saying (you better be saying!).

You can file what's known as an "83(b) election."

At a high level, the basics are this: under Section 83(b), the IRS allows the recipient to make an election. She can do nothing and defer the tax hits until vesting while gambling that the value stays low. Not advisable in Startupland.

Or she can elect to treat the stock as fully vested, right now. So even though the stock has yet to actually vest, she is willing to ignore that in exchange for the opportunity to pay the tax in full, now. Why would she do that? Why would anyone ever want to accelerate a tax obligation? Because the tax is calculated on current value. In our example, $60 rather than $6,000,000. Whew.

Two key points:

- An 83(b) election must be filed with the IRS no later than 30 days after the date of stock issuance. THIS IS HARD AND FAST. Don't blow it!
- 83(b) elections only apply to restricted shares (inapplicable to options), and only restricted shares subject to vesting (inapplicable to fully vested shares).

Well, that was fun . . .

. . . I know, and thank you for your patience! Like that whole Delaware par value discussion early on, it's a bit technical, and it feels overly detailed and granular for a big picture book like this, but I elected (heh) to include this discussion, like the franchise tax discussion, because the consequences are incredibly profound and important.

I hope that softens the blow and leaves you a little less irritated with me . . .

31

Number and Price

So that pretty much does it for vesting! Yay!

So now that we have knocked that out, let's hammer through the other key provisions of an option: namely, the number of shares and the exercise price.

32

Coverage

I felt like we needed a short chapter after that vesting slog!

Options tend to arise in one of two places.

They are awarded as equity compensation for services rendered or to be rendered. Like to employees. Here they are usually called options. And they almost always vest. These are the circumstances on which we've been focused since Chapter 25. Let's call these "service options."

But there is another context, too, and it's equally important.

Namely, options can also be included as part of an investment transaction as an extra "kicker." Sometimes people call it "juice," sometimes "deal grease." I know—pretty exciting terminology for finance types! Here, they are usually called "warrants," not options, and we'll refer to them as "investment warrants."

The basic idea behind investment warrants is that the investor, for whatever reason, wants something more than just the investment instrument it is directly purchasing. Those preferred shares or that convertible seed note, for instance, just don't give the investor everything it wants. Maybe the investor is suffering from the dreaded hedonic assimilation . . .

(Note: investment warrants rarely vest. The idea is that the investor has already "performed" simply by writing a check for the related investment instrument. It's all the investor was asked to do. So the investor should be able to enjoy the warrant in full, right now.)

With this wind in our sails, let's get into the number of shares for which an option or warrant is exercisable. Sometimes this is called "coverage."

With respect to service options, what most companies do is develop "bands." That is, they will stratify their aspirational, current, and future employees into groups, and then apply to each group a range of equity ownership. This is one place where the internet actually does include a lot of good market information. Ask your trusted advisors as well.

For instance, in many companies, a typical peg for director-level employees is 0.25% of total equity. So these individuals would be issued options (or perhaps restricted shares, if we are still in the early low-value days) representative of that amount of ownership.

As for investment warrants, a signifying percentage is typically used as well, but it references a completely different figure. You may see a term sheet, for instance, where the investor is investing $1,000,000 in a convertible seed note and is also receiving "20% warrant coverage."

It may be 5%, it could be 50%, but just like convertible seed note discounts are usually 20%, so too warrant coverage. I don't think this was an accident. I think the numeral "2" on someone's keyboard was stuck. In any event . . .

Here, in the context of investment warrants, the percentage relates to the amount invested. So in our example, 20% warrant coverage in the context of a $1,000,000 convertible seed note would mean that the investor will receive warrants representing the right to purchase $200,000 in warrant shares.

This, of course, raises the question, how many shares represent "$200,000 in warrant shares"?

Well, you know the answer!

It all ties back to the equations we have rinsed and repeated throughout this book:

$$\frac{\text{PRE-MONEY VALUATION}}{\text{PRE-MONEY TOTAL SHARES}} = \text{PRICE PER SHARE (PPS)}$$

$$\frac{\text{INVESTMENT AMOUNT}}{\text{PPS}} = \text{\# OF SHARES SOLD}$$

Here, the "investment amount" is the total value of the warrant shares. In our example, $200,000.

If this is a "priced round," this is easy. What's that, you say? Well, a priced round means that the company is selling preferred shares. We are determining a "price." And we can use that price not only to tell us how many preferred shares the investor is buying but also the number of warrant shares. Whatever price is used to determine the number of preferred shares purchased is also used to determine the number of warrant shares.

But what if it's not a priced round? What if, say, the warrant is attached to a convertible seed note?

In that case, the warrant share calculation ties back to the convertible seed note. It would say something to the effect of, hey, you know that convertible seed note? It will convert, at some point, at some price per share (might have a discount, might be tied to a cap—or not). Whatever that price per share is for purposes of that conversion, that price per share will tell us the number of warrant shares available.

So if our warrant coverage is 20%, and if that means $200,000 in warrant shares—and if the convertible seed note ultimately converts into preferred shares at a price per share of $2.00, say—then the warrant will be exercisable for 100,000 of those same preferred shares ($200,000 / $2).

Got it?

33

Price

What do you mean, price? Weren't we just talking about price?

Yes, we were. But in a specific context. Namely, in the context of determining the NUMBER of warrant shares for which an investment warrant is exercisable.

But we haven't addressed the more significant pricing question—at what PRICE is the option or warrant itself actually exercisable? In other words, what price per share must the holder PAY the company to receive the underlying shares?

What's the purchase price, or exercise price, or strike price?

There is a spectrum, but in most cases, you'll see one of two approaches. Either current fair market value, or $0.01.

Let's start with fair market value, or FMV. In most cases, service options must be priced at current FMV. That's generally required by Section 422 of the Internal Revenue Code (in the case of options known as "incentive stock options") or Section 409A (the case of options known as "non-qualified stock options"). If you have heard people bandying about the phrase "409A valuation," this is what they are getting at.

The point is—the company is valued. And that value is inserted as the "pre-money valuation" in the first equation of our handy-dandy equation set. A "price per share" results—and that's our strike price.

Hmmm, you may think. What's the big deal then? You are giving someone the right to buy stock at its current value. Doesn't seem very interesting. "Hey, a baseball card costs $1.00. Here's an option which represents a right to buy it for $1.00." Snooze.

Well, it's a big deal for two reasons.

First, recall the tax discussion around restricted shares. Remember how we said they are immediately taxable at current FMV because the recipient is getting value right now? In the case of options, because they are only receiving the right to buy something at its current value, the option itself is not deemed to have current value for tax purposes. In other words, the receipt of an option like this is tax-free at award. Yay!

This is also why options, and not restricted shares, become the instrument of choice as company value grows.

But wait, there's more . . .

Yes, receiving the right to buy something at current FMV is not exciting today. But it may be tomorrow—because the exercise price is fixed.

So let's return to my baseball card example. If that baseball card is expected to rise in value to $4.00 in 4 years, having a right to buy it at $1.00 may not be exciting now, but it sure will be in 4 years.

Same with a service option. If the stock is valued at $2.00 per share today, well fine. But if it's worth $10.00 per share in 4 years, the recipient will be able to buy something worth $10.00 for $2.00. Netting, in effect, $8.00 in value for themselves. Yay!

Ok, so that's FMV. But what about $0.01. That sounds awesome and even better!

Using the example above, let's say the stock today is worth $2.00 per share. Instead of an option priced at $2.00 per share, you get a warrant priced at $0.01. Whoa! You are already making money. Yay!

These are called "in-the-money," because they are already worth something. And because they are already worth something, in most contexts, including service options, their very issuance would generally result in immediate tax—and there may also be a penalty tax under the Internal Revenue Code. Boo!

But . . .

In the context of an investment transaction, the company may be able to issue so-called "penny warrants" to an investor. Facts and circumstances matter, so proceed with caution, but frequently, because the issuance arises in an investment and not in a compensation context, it hits a different section of the tax code and isn't taxable. Yay!

So yes, investment warrants can indeed be priced at current FMV. And they often are. But you can bet that if it is able, an investor's starting position will be to ask for an exercise price of $0.01. And like any negotiation—where we negotiate valuation, discount, cap, participating preferred versus non-participating preferred, or whatever—that may be the ultimate outcome.

Which would mean the investor would only need to pay $0.01 per share to acquire its warrant shares.

So now you see why these investment warrants can be very attractive "deal grease." If the investor is not fully satisfied with the terms of its basic investment instrument—whether preferred shares or a convertible seed note or whatever—it may ask for a warrant. A warrant priced at current FMV is nice, for the very reasons a service option priced at current FMV is nice. The hope is the value goes up, and locking in this price today is economically beneficial. But a price of $0.01 is even better! So don't be surprised to see that ask.

34

Types of Stock Options

In Chapter 33, we mentioned in passing the two types of service options: namely, "incentive stock options" and "non-qualified stock options." The differences between the two deserve a bit more color.

Incentive stock options are sometimes called "ISOs." People often mistakenly think that ISOs refer to all options, especially all service options. This is not true. To qualify as incentive stock options, the option must satisfy the criteria of Section 422 of the Internal Revenue Code.

Of these various criteria, three leap off the page. One is the current FMV requirement noted above (and for some recipients, the Code requires that the exercise price be set at 110% of current FMV). The other two? Only corporations may award ISOs, and ISOs may only be awarded to W-2 employees.

Beyond the pricing requirements set forth in Section 409A of the Internal Revenue Code, non-qualified stock options have very few limitations. They may be awarded by any type of entity, to any type of recipient.

I've always felt a bit sorry for non-qualified stock options. They are named as such simply because they don't "qualify" as ISOs. My name is David. It would be as if your name were "Not David." Bummer, right?

Ok, so back to the matter at hand. Why do we even care about the ISO vs. NQSO distinction?

Reason: taxes.

Generally speaking, and assuming the strike prices are calculated and set appropriately, neither ISOs nor NQSOs are taxable to the recipient on award. Yay!

With any option, there are two phases.

The first phase—phase 1—runs between the date of the actual award of the option, and the date on which the option is actually exercised and the underlying option shares purchased.

The second phase—phase 2—runs between that exercise date and the date on which the purchased shares are actually sold.

It can be illustrated like this:

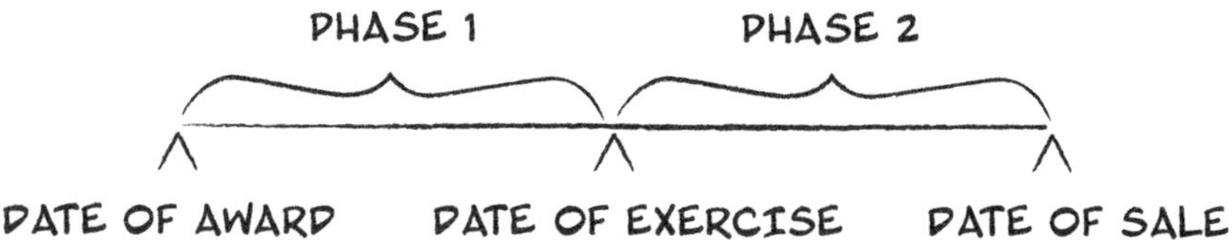

With NQSOs, the holder is taxed on *exercise*. In other words, at the end of phase 1, on the phase 1 gain. The gain is calculated by subtracting the strike price from the actual per-share fair market value of the shares on that date. And as if that weren't bad enough, the tax is calculated at ordinary rates and not at capital gains rates (the latter are generally lower).

This can be highly inconvenient in Startupland. Recall our conversation about restricted shares, and how there are limits placed on transferability? Well, limits of that sort apply to most shares issued by startups—and regardless, even without such restrictions, there generally isn't much of a market for these shares yet anyway. So even if you could technically sell the shares, there aren't really any buyers.

All of which means that it's highly improbable that the holder of an NQSO will be able to sell some of the shares she just bought to cover the tax liability. She'll need to pull that cash from another bucket. Like I said, highly inconvenient.

This is the big benefit of ISOs. On exercise? No tax. No tax payable on that phase 1 gain at this point. Talk about a yay!

What happens next? Well, in the case of both NQSOs and ISOs, the holder must indeed pay tax at the time they sell the option shares. In other words, at the end of phase 2.

Despite that default rule, that phase 1 gain is a preference item for the alternative minimum tax (AMT). What's AMT? Basically, some people got really good at tax loopholes, and so the government put in place the AMT to ensure they at least pay something. That's enough to know for purposes of this book.

In the case of an ISO, the tax is based on the difference between the strike price and the price at which the shares were actually sold. In other words, the full gain, taking into account both phase 1 and phase 2. And, assuming the holding periods are satisfied (more on this below), the gain is taxed at the applicable capital gains tax rate.

In the case of an NQSO, the tax is based on the phase 2 gain only, calculated as the difference between the fair market value of the shares on the date of exercise and the price at which the shares were actually sold. Why only phase 2? Because the holder already paid the tax on the phase 1 gain.

With an NQSO, if the holder has held the shares long enough, that tax on the phase 2 gain can qualify and be calculated at the applicable long-term capital gains rate. That lessens the blow.

To return to our illustration above, we can summarize these tax matters this way:

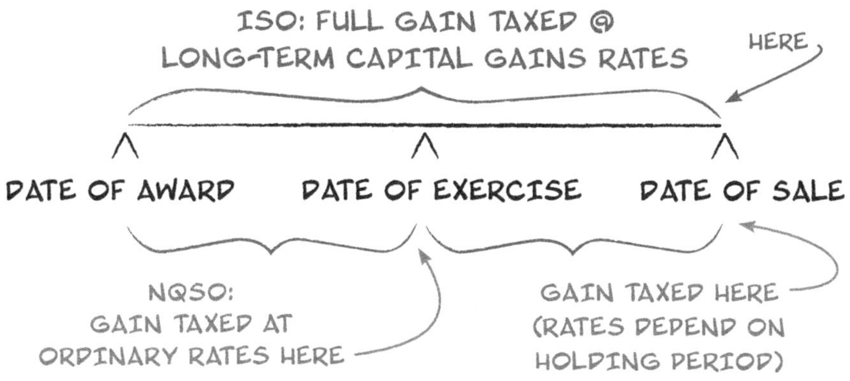

So is that it? Not quite. Because a funny thing happens on the way to the forum . . .

Because holders of NQSOs are obligated to pay tax at exercise, they typically won't exercise until they know they can turn right around immediately and sell at least some of the shares they just bought. They just don't have that other bucket of cash laying around that they can draw from to pay Uncle Sam.

But wait, didn't we say that it's hard to sell these shares?

Yes, yes we did. Thanks for paying attention.

But there does indeed come a time when it is viable.

When?

When the company is sold! The liquidity event! The exit transaction!

So the holder of an NQSO will typically wait until that moment to exercise. Then she'll immediately dispose of those shares in connection with the exit. So her phase 1 is looooooong. And her phase 2 is infinitesimally short. We know the phase 1 gain is taxed at ordinary rates regardless. And with phase 2 being so short, because the long-term capital gains holding period requirements are nowhere near being satisfied, the gain in that phase is taxed at short-term capital gains rates (which are generally equal to ordinary rates).

In other words . . .

Practically speaking in Startupland, holders of NQSOs will wait to exercise those options until the exit. And at that time, they'll pay tax, at ordinary rates, on the full gain as measured between the strike price and the price at which the option shares were actually sold.

So ISOs seem ideal, right? No tax at exercise regardless, and the full gain is taxed at the applicable long-term capital gains rate. Boom. Way better than NQSOs.

Well, not so fast.

Even though holders of ISOs don't need to pay regular TAX at exercise (but don't forget about AMT), they still need to pay the actual strike price. They still need to buy the dang shares from the company.

And perhaps not surprisingly, they don't want to pull that trigger until they know the shares will actually be worth something. Seems sensible.

Well, when is that moment?

You know the answer: the exit, of course!

So like holders of NQSOs, most holders of ISOs in Startupland will wait to exercise their options until the very moment in which they can turn around and dispose of the purchased shares. Seems smart, right?

Well, kinda.

From an investment perspective, sure. Who doesn't like a sure thing? But there is a problem.

You know how I said Section 422 of the Internal Revenue Code sets forth a whole bunch of criteria respecting ISOs? Well, in addition to the three I noted above, there is another criterion which goes to holding period.

Uh oh . . .

That's right. To maintain qualification, the shares may not be sold within two years of the date on which the actual ISO was originally awarded.

Frankly, this requirement tends not to be a big deal, and is usually satisfied with ease.

But wait, there's more . . .

The shares may also not be sold within . . . one year of . . . (wait for it) . . . the date of exercise.

Uh oh, is right.

So waiting may make sense from a certainty-of-gain perspective, but it blows the ISO qualification. A sale under these circumstances is called a "disqualifying disposition," and as a consequence, the ISO is treated as an NQSO. See above . . .

That's a whole lot of words to basically just say this: in Startupland, the benefits of ISOs are rarely realized. Instead, regardless of original designation, virtually all service options tend to end up in the NQSO bucket, tend to be exercised in connection with the exit, and as a consequence, tend to have the full gain taxed at ordinary rates.

Whew. That was kind of a lot. But still, aren't you glad you asked?

(I actually didn't ask, you are saying . . .)

SECTION 409A

Section 409A of the Internal Revenue Code has been referenced a few times in this book. It's an expansive provision relating to all kinds of compensation programs. We care here about Section 409A because it reaches non-qualified stock options.

Generally speaking, Section 409A requires that NQSOs be priced at current FMV. It permits that pricing to be determined in one of two ways. Either experts within the company itself can determine current FMV, or a third-party resource can determine the price. In either case, the company's Board will ultimately review, approve, and apply the recommended value.

What's the key difference? Simply put, an outside appraisal is more likely to stick. Yes, Section 409A does permit home-grown valuations. And if done in complete conformity with the rule, they are every bit as definitive as an outside appraisal.

But, in the home-grown case, Section 409A requires that the valuation be performed by a person within the company with "significant knowledge, experience, education, or training" and goes on to add that "significant experience generally means at least five years of relevant experience in business valuation or appraisal, financial accounting, investment banking, private equity, secured lending, or other comparable experience in the line of business or industry in which the service recipient operates."

That person rarely exists in a startup, especially a seed-stage startup.

Does it matter? Well, if the IRS comes a-knocking, and if a third-party report was relied upon, then the IRS must prove that the valuation was WRONG. Period. And the IRS has the same burden if instead of a third-party report, the Board relied on a home-grown valuation which passes muster. But if the company took that home-grown approach, and if the IRS pokes a hole in the experience of the person who performed it or the methodology she used, then the burden is on the company to prove that the valuation was RIGHT.

Seems academic, no? You'd be surprised. So often in legal disputes, regardless of the facts, the party with the burden of proof loses. So this difference in treatment matters. And it matters so much that Boards have a strong bias for third-party reports. Simply for the sake of certainty.

Final point: investors do not use or rely on 409A valuations when valuing a startup for investment purposes. They have a completely different perspective and outlook on things, and they view their process as apples to the oranges of Section 409A.

Final final point: while Section 409A does not generally apply to ISOs or to restricted shares, you'll frequently see 409A valuations cited and used in those contexts. Why? Simply because the 409A process is generally the most rigorous, and because maintaining valuation harmony across all types and forms of equity compensation is helpful and desirable.

35

What Kind of Shares?

As we discussed wayyyyyyyyyy earlier in this book, shares issued for services are almost always common shares. Options work the same way. Service options are almost always structured as the right to purchase common shares.

What about warrants in an investment transaction? These can be preferred. Again, consistent with what we noted above—preferred shares are the instrument of choice for money investors.

That said, if the startup doesn't yet have any preferred shares (as might be the case if its original seed deal is structured as a convertible seed note), then it would not be unusual to see a warrant for common shares. In other words, this is a place—perhaps the only place—in Startupland where a money investor may acquire something which ultimately converts into common shares. Everything else they purchase—whether directly or through conversion—is almost always preferred shares.

36

Homestretch!

Let me take you alllllll the way back to Chapter 24.

Remember this statement?

> *Preferred shares may be preferred shares, and convertible seed notes may have pretty well frozen into a stable instrument, but that doesn't mean that there aren't other new market entrants.*
>
> *But wait, how can that be?*
>
> *Convertible seed notes are debt. Preferred shares are equity. Those are the two—and only two—quadrants on the righthand side of the balance sheet. There's no room for anything else, right?*
>
> *Wrong.*

And then we took this looooooong detour through equity compensation.

Sorry, not sorry. For two reasons:

First, at the end of the day, this book is all about the cap table. It's all about understanding the inputs and the outputs, and the impact and importance of each. Issuing equity to employees is every bit as significant as issuing equity to investors. So it's good and necessary to understand how that works.

And now you do!

But second, I teased a “new market entrant.” What’s that?

The SAFE.

37

SAFEs Introduced

The safe was invented in Egypt in the 13th century BCE.

Um . . .

Oh, wait. Different safe.

The SAFE was invented in 2013 by Y Combinator, a top-tier accelerator on the West Coast.

For the uninitiated, an "accelerator" is a hothouse for startups. I am frequently asked whether I am "for" or "against" accelerators. I am neither, or rather, I am both. I am "for" good accelerators, and I am "against" bad accelerators. That's a radical stance, eh? But they are like anything—consider your situation. Maybe an accelerator would help, maybe not. If you think it would help, go find a good one. Don't just join the first one that accepts you. Kick the tires. Do your homework.

Anyhow, back to SAFEs.

"SAFE" is an acronym. It stands for "Simple Agreement for Future Equity" (or sometimes just "Simple Agreement For Equity"). Ok, fine. That tells us little. What are these things?

Well, let's create an inventory of what we have covered and discussed in this book and see if we can tease it out.

A balance sheet has two quadrants on the righthand side. Liabilities and Equity.

Convertible seed notes live in the Liabilities quadrant, at least until they convert into shares. When they convert into shares, they become Equity. Because Equity is where shares reside.

What kinds of shares reside there? All of the kinds: common shares and preferred shares.

Common shares in the form of restricted shares or founder shares hang out there. The preferred shares purchased by investors do as well. And so, too, do the common shares purchased on the exercise of service options, and the shares (whether common or preferred) purchased on the exercise of investment warrants.

And finally—options and warrants are themselves tucked in there.

So what about SAFEs?

38

Background

SAFEs, like convertible seed notes, are convertible instruments. They convert into, they are exercisable for, shares. Because they are acquired by investors, the shares are preferred shares.

Recall that convertible seed notes originally entered the scene as a solution to the problem of valuation. At a time when valuations were notoriously hard to negotiate (the dotcom era), the convertible seed note represented a fix. Investors could invest through these instruments, no valuation needed to be discussed or finalized, and then when that proverbial Qualified Financing popped, and the company sold preferred shares to new money investors, the convertible seed notes would convert into preferred shares—using that valuation.

At first it was the same valuation, and then we saw the introduction of the discount. Eventually, the cap appeared—which, as we noted, did indeed represent the reintroduction of valuation, smuggled in through the backdoor.

But that was ok because, at this point, Startupland had evolved, and due to information and data and experience, valuations (or caps) could be teased out.

So why still use a convertible seed note? Why not retire it completely, and just return to preferred shares as the form of seed deals?

Some investors did indeed move that way, and "Seed Preferred Shares" or "Series Seed Preferred Shares" are well-defined and popular means of investment.

But the convertible seed note proved sticky, and it stuck around. Not because of the original rationale (valuation bottlenecks), but because they are simple and easy.

Principal amount, interest rate, and maturity date. Discount and/or cap. That's it. Sort those out, and you are done. That simplicity is elegant, and convenient—and cheap.

Well, Y Combinator, like a lot of accelerators and participants in Startupland, certainly appreciated those convertible seed note attributes. But they and others did point out two problems with convertible seed notes.

It's beyond the scope of this book, but the treatment of interest accrued and earned on convertible seed notes, especially upon conversion into preferred shares, can create some tax challenges. Arguably it is income to the investor, at that moment, because the preferred shares represent the payment of interest for tax purposes (many accountants say, whoa, not "arguably"—it just is!).

Remember our discussion of equity compensation? Paying tax on the exercise of NQSOs is not fun because you haven't really cashed a check yet. Any gain is just on paper. People just don't like to spend money on taxes until they have a real "cash in the bank" gain to which they can point. Same thing here.

So interest is a little tricky. You said two issues, you may be thinking. What's the other one?

Maturity date. If the maturity date is reached before conversion, well, at least in theory, the convertible seed note is due—the company must repay principal and interest in cash.

We spilled a lot of ink in a lot of places and contexts around why this is terrifying for startups. It's highly unlikely that they'll have the cash on hand to satisfy this obligation. Recall that was the objection to simple seed notes, our infant version of this instrument. And relatedly, because they can't pay up, they need the convertible seed note holder to agree to some kind of accommodation—an extension, forbearance, something.

This is directly analogous to the non (Non) Qualified Financing scenario. The company needs something from the convertible seed note holder (here, an extension; there, the voluntary agreement to convert). Sometimes the convertible seed note holder is happy to comply. In fact, I would say far more often than not this is the case.

But sometimes they are not so inclined. Maybe the company has not treated them well. Maybe the founders have been unresponsive and uncommunicative. Maybe the convertible seed note holder is a jerk. Maybe a little bit of all of this.

Regardless, in this situation, the company will need to give to get. What can it give to get this accommodation?

Maybe a greater discount. Maybe a lower cap. Maybe an investment warrant priced at $0.01. Maybe a little bit of all of this.

But bottom line—many in the space believe that maturity dates by and large create a distorted moment on the startup timeline, a situation where startups and their founders could be held hostage by the convertible seed note holders and forced to surrender big chunks of economics. It feels unfair.

39

The SAFE Itself

So the idea is this:

Convertible seed notes are elegantly simple. But the interest rate and maturity date components can be hairy.

So what if instead we just take a convertible seed note and strip out those two things? And call it a SAFE. And we'll give founders and investors alternatives.

(And Y Combinator did. You can go to the website and download a SAFE with a discount and a cap. With no discount and no cap. With a discount and no cap. Or with no discount and a cap.)

Huzzah!

But what the heck is this beast?

It's not debt—it's not a note—for the very reason that it doesn't include an interest rate or a maturity date. Recall that in our discussion of seed notes, we noted that these two elements are required for an instrument to qualify as debt. So SAFEs are not debt. Which means they cannot be situated in the Liabilities quadrant of the balance sheet.

Which leaves us with Equity. But what kind of Equity?

SAFEs are not common shares or preferred shares—at least not yet.

What are they? Well, they are convertible into, they are exercisable for, preferred shares. When? In connection with a Qualified Financing (or with the SAFE holder's consent, a non (Non) Qualified Financing).

What else, besides convertible seed notes, do startups sometimes issue to investors which are convertible into—or exercisable for—preferred shares?

You got it. Investment warrants.

That's what a SAFE is. It's an investment warrant. But unlike the investment warrants we have discussed to this point, which have been attached to or associated with an investment in something else (usually preferred shares or a convertible seed note), SAFEs stand on their own two feet.

And interestingly, unlike typical investment warrants, the purchase price for the underlying preferred shares—the exercise price—is paid up front.

Generally speaking, with investment warrants, as well as with service options, the option or warrant is simply issued to the recipient without an expectation of cash payment for the underlying shares at that time. Instead, the cash payment is made—the purchase price/exercise price/strike price is paid—when the option or warrant is actually exercised and the shares actually purchased.

In the case of a SAFE, that cash payment is paid up front. It's paid at the time of issuance. It's analogous to the principal amount of a convertible seed note. The SAFE itself is actually exercised—converted into preferred shares—not when the holder pays the purchase price for the shares (they already did that) but when the Qualified Financing (or non (Non) Qualified Financing) takes place.

It's as . . . (wait for it) . . . SIMPLE . . . as that.

Heh.

40

Pre-Money versus Post-Money SAFEs

The first version of SAFEs was "pre-money." The current version of SAFEs is "post-money." Why the change? What's the difference?

I considered skipping this discussion, and if you have simply had it with me, feel free to do so. It can get a little technical, and we are back in the math. But I ultimately decided to include this material both because it's highly relevant in Startupland and because it will act as a sort of summation of virtually everything we have covered in this book. It's a nice runway on which to land this plane.

Ok, here we go:

Traditionally, convertible instruments—whether convertible seed notes or SAFEs—have been pre-money. This goes to the cap and rolls through our tried-and-true equations:

$$\frac{\text{PRE-MONEY VALUATION}}{\text{PRE-MONEY TOTAL SHARES}} = \text{PRICE PER SHARE (PPS)}$$

$$\frac{\text{INVESTMENT AMOUNT}}{\text{PPS}} = \text{\# OF SHARES SOLD}$$

The cap stands in for pre-money valuation, as we know. Ok, fine. What's the big deal?

Well, the big deal is this:

Consider our initial cap table:

	SHARES	%	
A	6M	60%	
B	3M	30%	
C	1M	10%	
	10M	100%	

Remember that? Ah, yes. Those early chapters. Such an innocent time . . .

Let's say our original investor invested $100,000 in a pre-money SAFE with a cap of $4,500,000. And let's say its expectation was that the total

SAFE round—in other words, inclusive of all the SAFEs to be sold to it and to all other investors—would be $500,000.

In that case, our original investor may be walking around thinking that it will end-up owning 2% of the company. Why?

Remember this?

PRE-MONEY VALUATION
+ INVESTMENT AMOUNT

POST-MONEY VALUATION

If the pre-money valuation—or the cap—is $4,500,000, and the investment amount is $500,000, then the post-money valuation is $5,000,000.

And $500,000 / $5,000,000 = 10%. Which means $100,000 would equal 2%.

Ok, seems about right. Is it?

Not really.

First, remember that these SAFEs will be converting in connection with a new money financing—whether a Qualified Financing or a non (Non) Qualified Financing. And while, ok, perhaps our original investor will hold 2% of the company for a moment in time, that 2% will be diluted by the impact of the new money investors. But there is something else to be wary of, too. Read on . . .

Ok, to take this in, let's run out the example a bit further. We have $500,000 in SAFEs with a $5,000,000 cap. Let's say our financing was $5,000,000 in new money, on a pre-money valuation of $10,000,000. We'll calculate the SAFE conversion first, and then the new money investment.

(Note: we often run the new money math first, because our convertible seed note or SAFE will often have, as an alternative to the cap, a discount. And to calculate a discount, we need the new money price per share figure.)

SAFES

$$\frac{\$4{,}500{,}000}{10{,}000{,}000} = \$0.45 \text{ PPS}$$

$$\frac{\$500{,}000}{\$0.45} = 1{,}111{,}111 \text{ SHARES}$$

NEW $

$$\frac{\$10{,}000{,}000}{10{,}000{,}000} = \$1.00 \text{ PPS}$$

$$\frac{\$5{,}000{,}000}{\$1.00} = 5{,}000{,}000 \text{ SHARES}$$

So our cap table:

	COMMON	PREFERRED	TOTAL	%
A	6M	–	6M	37.24%
B	3M	–	3M	18.62%
C	1M	–	1M	6.20%
SAFE	–	1,111,111	1,111,111	6.90%
NEW $	–	5,000,000	5,000,000	31.04%
	10,000,000	6,111,111	16,111,111	100.00%

Ugly! All that early simplicity, gone. Pour one out . . .

A little recap (heh)—you'll see the dilution incurred by our Founder A. She started at 60%. Now, after two financings, she sits at 37.24%. That's a lot of dilution. On the other hand, she also raised $5,500,000 in total. So hopefully, that $5,500,000 will fuel her and her co-founders to big growth and big value appreciation, making it all worthwhile!

Also note that in converting the SAFEs, we didn't need to fool with interest. It was just $500,000. A little simpler than convertible seed notes, where we would have needed to incorporate that input (and it's a pain because it grows literally daily and requires constant refreshment in the days leading up to conversion).

Including the 5,000,000 preferred shares sold to the new money investors, our SAFE holders now sit at 6.90%. But if we were to do the math in advance of that, it would look like this:

$$1{,}111{,}111 \,/\, 11{,}111{,}111 = 10\%$$

And so our original investor, having invested $100,000 of that $500,000, would have indeed been sitting at 2%. After the impact of the new money shares, of course, that 2% becomes 1.38%.

This is how the math of a pre-money SAFE works.

For starters, our original investor could not have reasonably expected to sit at 2% on any sort of durable basis. Why? Because that 2% is not actually realized until the new money financing, which is immediately dilutive.

But even beyond that, there is another issue. That 2% expectation was not only calculated in a vacuum (because it didn't take the new money financing into account), but it also assumed a SAFE round of $500,000.

What if the SAFE round went to $600,000? Or $700,000? Or $1,000,000?

Well, let's say it did go to $1,000,000. Our equation would look like this:

$$\begin{array}{r} \$4{,}500{,}000 \\ +\ \$1{,}000{,}000 \\ \hline \$5{,}500{,}000 \end{array}$$

And $1,000,000 / $5,500,000 = 18.18%. Our original investor contributed $100,000 of that $1,000,000, or 10%. So their ownership percentage would be 1.82%.

Hmmmm. Lower than 2%.

In other words, original investors in pre-money SAFEs have very little visibility into where their ultimate ownership percentage will end up. The size of the new money financing most certainly matters. But so too does the size of the SAFE round matter.

And that variability—oftentimes showing up with downward pressure on ownership—irritated a lot of these investors.

We have seen this before. And the result is always the same—irritated investors force change. And that happened here as well.

Entrance: The post-money SAFE.

These are easy. Sorta.

The cap is expressed on a post-money basis. And it includes the full SAFE round—no matter how large.

Which means that, in our example, NO MATTER HOW MUCH SAFE MONEY IS RAISED, a $100,000 SAFE converts into preferred shares representing a 2% ownership interest in the company. Not 1.82%, or anything else.

It's important to note that the final, "when the dust settles" ownership interest in the company will still be diluted by the new money. That's not avoided.

But what is avoided is the chipping away which can occur if SAFE rounds grow beyond their original anticipated size.

So let's return to our example once again. If our SAFE is a pre-money SAFE with a $4,500,000 pre-money cap, and if $500,000 is raised under SAFEs, it looks like this:

PRE-MONEY VALUATION (CAP)	$4,500,000
+ INVESTMENT AMOUNT (TOTAL)	$500,000
POST-MONEY VALUATION	$5,000,000
	SAFES = 10%

What if instead our SAFE is a post-money SAFE with a $5,000,000 pre-money cap, and if $500,000 is raised under SAFEs?

Well, it looks like this:

	POST-MONEY VALUATION (CAP)	$5,000,000
-	INVESTMENT AMOUNT (TOTAL)	$500,000
	PRE-MONEY VALUATION	$4,500,000
		SAFES = 10%

In other words, it's exactly the same. But what if the SAFE round grew to $1,000,000? Well . . .

PRE-MONEY SAFE:

	PRE-MONEY VALUATION (CAP)	$4,500,000
+	INVESTMENT AMOUNT (TOTAL)	$1,000,000
	POST-MONEY VALUATION	$5,500,000
		SAFES = 18.18%

POST-MONEY SAFE:

	POST-MONEY VALUATION (CAP)	$5,000,000
-	INVESTMENT AMOUNT (TOTAL)	$1,000,000
	PRE-MONEY VALUATION	$4,000,000
		SAFES = 20%

What did we learn? Under a post-money SAFE, a $100,000 investment will result in a 2% ownership interest no matter what. It will always be $100,000 / $5,000,000 = 2%.

In a pre-money SAFE, it will vary, based upon the amount raised. If more than the anticipated amount, then the $100,000 will end up less than 2%. Interestingly enough, however, if the company raises less than the anticipated amount, then the $100,000 SAFE may end up representing more than 2%.

While that latter possibility is tantalizing for investors, they realized that far more often, more, and not less, money is raised.

Consequently, with increasing frequency, led by the example of Y Combinator, investors in SAFEs are opting for the post-money variety.

This is not the end of the world for founders. It simply means that they must be disciplined and mindful about how much they raise. And understand that the more they raise, the more they will dilute themselves.

How? Well, in our example, the pre-money SAFE had a fixed $4,500,000 cap. That means that the founders, regardless of the size of the SAFE round, will always fit into $4,500,000.

But with a post-money SAFE, the founders live in whatever is left after the SAFEs are accounted for. So in our example, because $1,000,000 rather than $500,000 was raised, the founders saw themselves squeezed down from a $4,500,000 pre-money valuation to a $4,000,000 pre-money valuation.

Again, it's not the end of the world. These founders raised $1,000,000 rather than $500,000. That could be a great thing! It just means that the founders need to understand the ramifications of their decisions on ownership and intentionally choose the course they take. If more money is necessary, and available, and if they believe that the extra dilution is worth it because of the long-term value that can be created—then by all means, take it!

SECURITIES LAWS

Any time a startup sells or awards common shares or preferred shares (or convertible instruments like options, warrants, convertible seed notes, or SAFEs), it issues a "security."

When discussing the Delaware "C" corporation, we noted that in the United States, corporate law is primarily a function of state law. There is very little federal corporate law. So we look to the states when we look for guidance around the organization and governance of corporations.

We have also mentioned the Internal Revenue Code (IRC) a few times. That's federal law, and it applies in many contexts. While we haven't paid any mind to it, it's good to note that state tax laws are generally triggered when the IRC is triggered.

Securities laws work the same way. When considering the issuance by a company of new securities, the primary applicable statute is the Securities Act of 1933 (the "1933 Act"). We'll look at that here in a moment. But like with the tax laws, don't lose sight of state securities laws as well. They are implicated.

Under the 1933 Act, any issuance of securities must be registered with the Securities and Exchange Commission (SEC) unless an exemption applies. We are highly motivated to find exemptions because registration is expensive and time-consuming. Fortunately, there are several, and particularly in a company's early days, it's fairly easy to find one or more that fit.

Here are four good ones. The first three are tied to something called "Regulation D" (the cool kids sometimes call it Reg D). These are rules that the SEC created themselves under power delegated to them under the 1933 Act.

1. Rule 504 of Reg D. This provision works well if the startup is raising from both accredited and non-accredited investors. But there's a hard cap at $10,000,000.

(What does it mean to be an "accredited investor"? There are many ways to qualify under Reg D, but for individuals, the focus is typically on their income or their net worth. If they exceed a certain level, they are "accredited.")

2. Rule 506(b) of Reg D. This provision allows a startup to raise an unlimited amount of money from an unlimited number of accredited investors, but if the company includes non-accredited investors in the offering, the disclosure requirements are significantly elevated (result: it just costs the company more legal dollars to get the job done).

(Furthermore, under both Rules 504 and 506(b), "general solicitation" is prohibited. This simply means that the company cannot broadly market the offering to strangers.)

3. Rule 506(c) of Reg D. This provision permits general solicitation, which can be quite attractive, particularly in these times of social media where startups can broadcast widely at very little cost. But the trade-off is that all the investors must be accredited, and these investors must provide objective verification of this status (under Rule 506(b), in constrast, they can just self-verify by checking a box). This may seem like a small thing, but it's a big hurdle. As a general matter, wealthy people value privacy and are loathe to share financial information.

(These three exemptions all require the filing of something called a "Form D" with the SEC. It's a short and simple form—but it's publicly available. Some founders hate this, especially when they want to remain in "stealth mode." They don't want the public to learn of their fundraising activities.)

For startups that want to remain truly stealth, or that may need some flexibility around the hard-and-fast accredited versus non-accredited classifications, Section 4(a)(2) of the 1933 Act is often a good fit. No filing is required, there is no cap on offering size, and its requirement that investors simply be "sophisticated" also offers a bit more maneuverability. That said, the prohibition on general solicitation applies here as well.

Remember the point about compliance with state securities laws as well? Well, that's absolutely required for companies relying on Rule 504 or on Section 4(a)(2). But it's NOT required under Rule 506(b) or 506(c). The technical term here is "preemption." The federal laws preempt the state laws. So that's a nice little bonus.

Not yet comatose? Good. a quick word on Rule 701 . . .

Options and warrants, like stock, are securities. So just like an exemption is necessary for stock sales, an exemption is also required for option awards and warrant issuances.

As a general matter, all the exemptions that we just discussed can be used for options and warrants as well. They are, as we have said, "securities" like any other. And these exemptions are indeed the place we look when we are talking about *investment warrants.*

But in the case of *service options*, most companies use a special rule that the SEC created specifically for compensatory arrangements like this: Rule 701.

To qualify, the service options must be awarded under a plan document that the company provides to the recipient. This is not a heavy lift, as Section 422 under the IRC already requires this for ISOs, and while not necessarily required for NQSOs, it's customarily done there as well. Bottom line, if you are awarding service options, you likely have this in place already.

There is a rolling 12-month cap on awards made under Rule 701. It's $1,000,000, and it's calculated on the basis of exercise price. Vesting schedules, and even the actual exercise itself, are disregarded. So if a recipient is awarded 100,000 options with a strike price of $1.00, that's a $100,000 issuance for Rule 701 purposes, even if none of the options is vested, and even if none of the options is ever exercised.

A company is permitted to exceed that $1,000,000 limitation if it satisfies certain formulas based on its assets or on the number of shares of common stock outstanding. Bigger companies will take advantage of those formulas. If the amount issued exceeds $10,000,000, certain additional disclosure to the recipients is required. If you are wrestling with that provision, then congratulations—you've made it! You've got a big company!

Finally, Rule 701 does not require a federal filing. Yay.

Ok, I lied. Not quite finally. Finally finally—and I promise, this is it—just as with the federal exemptions noted above, state securities laws cannot be ignored in the case of these compensatory arrangements. Most are a non-issue, but some, like California and New York, are a pain. Be attentive.

Conclusion

You made it!

I know it got tough in a few spots (more than a FEW, you may be thinking!). But you pressed ahead and got through it. And not just for the sake of saying you did, as some kind of startup rite of passage. I hope this book made you chuckle now and then, but this was ultimately not about entertainment.

The substance of this book is non-fiction, and it's meant to inform and educate you about a very important topic: how founders can stay on top of their cap table—understanding it, managing it, and ultimately using it to benefit themselves and their startup as a financial gas tank.

We covered a lot of ground. In the Introduction, I indexed the topics a bit, to make future reference simple. You've earned that right, and I hope you take advantage of it moving forward.

Good luck! And remember—don't hesitate to reach out if I can help:

David@SeedDeals.net

Index

Note to the Reader: This is not a "literal" index. Rather, I have endeavored to reference that page or those pages on which the noted term is meaningfully mentioned or used. For instance, I note seven page references for "Convertible Seed Note." That term appears far more often than that, of course. But in my estimation, for a reader seeking information specific to that term or concept, noting every aside or passing mention would not be useful. My objective was to be intentional and practical, not mechanical. I hope I have succeeded!